The Incidental Navigator

The Incidental Navigator

A Mauritian Navigator in Bomber Command

by Sir Maurice Rault QC

Edited by Sean Feast from a translation by Danielle Lagesse

This edition first published 2020 by Mention the War Ltd., 25 Cromwell Street, Merthyr Tydfil, CF47 8RY.

Originally published in French as Navigateur d'Occasion, 1985, by Best Graphics Ltd., Port Louis, Ille Maurice.

English translation of Navigateur d'Occasion © Danielle LAGESSE SA

This edition copyright 2020 © Sean Feast and Danielle Lagesse.

The right of Sean Feast and Danielle Lagesse to be identified as Authors of this work is asserted by them in accordance with the Copyright, Designs and Patents Act 1988.

All rights reserved. No part of this publication may be reproduced, stored in a retrieval system, transmitted in any form or by any means, electronic, mechanical or photocopied, recorded or otherwise, without the written permission of the publisher.

Cover design: Topics - The Creative Partnership www.topicsdesign.co.uk

Navigation chart courtesy of W/O Ken Staveley, RAFVR

A CIP catalogue reference for this book is available from the British Library.

ISBN 9781911255598

Dedication to:

Gérard Ythier (l) and Maurice Rault, whilst sergeants.

Flying Officer Gérard Ythier of Rose Hill, Mauritius – pilot - killed in action with 150 Squadron, 23rd February, 1945

Flight Sergeant Guy d'Assonville of Beau Bassin, Mauritius - wireless operator/air gunner - Killed on active service in Italy, 19th February 1945

Sergeant Hervé Rochecouste of Quatre Bornes, Mauritius - air gunner with 10 Squadron, killed in action 20th December 1943.

and

Henry Simms

Unacknowledged defenders of liberty.

Contents

Introduction 7
Chapter One - The Call 9
Chapter Two – Joining Up 14
Chapter Three - The Volunteer 18
Chapter Four – Canadian Adventure 25
Chapter Five - Finningley 33
Chapter Six – Into Battle 45
Chapter Seven – Elsham Wolds 50
Chapter Eight - Gravitation 68
Chapter Nine – The Zoo 78
Chapter Ten – Through Which Tortuous Pathways 86
Chapter Eleven – Futile Requiem 100
Chapter Twelve – Meanderings 105
Chapter Thirteen – Equinox 118
Chapter Fourteen – Clearer Skies 126
Chapter Fifteen – My First Peacetime Flight 130
Chapter Sixteen – Returning To Earth 133
Chapter Seventeen – Blue Grey Humour 136
Chapter Eighteen – My Burning Home 145
Epilogue 150
Addenda 153
   Maurice Rault – Operational Record 153
   Losses recorded by 103 Squadron in March 1945 155
Acknowledgements 160

Introduction

Maurice Rault

Maurice Rault was no ordinary Bomber Command navigator, and neither is this an ordinary memoir. Born on the small island of Mauritius, nuzzling in the Indian Ocean some 1,200 miles off the east African coast, Maurice is drawn by a love of two countries – Britain and France – to join the Royal Air Force (RAF) to help rid the continent of Nazi tyranny. He is also driven by a romantic ideal, and a sense of Chivalry from a previous age, to put right what he sees as a terrible wrong, a betrayal of France, and a burning passion to see the Allies prevail.

He follows his brother, Raymond, to Britain, and volunteers for aircrew. After initial training he is sent to Canada, marveling at its open skies and charmed by its beauty, before returning to a blacked-out Britain and the harsh reality of the bombing war against Germany. After converting to four engines he is eventually posted to 103 Squadron at Elsham Wolds and takes part in some of the final raids of the war, including a dramatic operation to Bremen which is nearly his last.

Although he completes comparatively few operations before being posted to Pathfinder Force (PFF), those few 'ops' have a profound effect on his view of life and his chances of survival. In a few short weeks, his Squadron loses eleven crews – more than seventy men – at a time when the Germans still fail to acknowledge they are beaten.

With other like-minded souls he is invited to join a secret society known as 'the zoo', to share with other intellectuals a love of books and culture as an escape from the horrors of war. There he meets 'Gilbert', Nestor, and the ill-fated

'Bigamist', who pushes his luck once too often and pays the ultimate price. Through these characters, and through the 'Toubib', Maurice reveals a different side to war, of compassion and love for men facing similar fears. Not everyone, we discover, overcomes such fears. Through the hideous 'Palmer' we learn of a different battle against one's inner soul, and the ultimate futility that even the love of a good woman cannot solve.

Maurice writes of the spirit of the Squadron, and of his crew, and the admiration and affection for 'the Butcher' who remains convinced that, given time and the resource, victory in Europe can be won by Bomber Command alone. He writes of the mundane, the pubs and the girls, and the Gremlins that appear to hide his pencil and lose his maps. He writes of his love for London, and his respect for a city that is bombed but never beaten, and that is so far removed from the green fields of Lincolnshire and Elsham as to be almost from an alien world. And he writes of the more profound, his discussion and debates with Gilbert's dying father, in a remote country house with its magnificent library on the merits of *Aeschylus*, and of his chance encounter with an SOE agent about to be dropped into France who escapes for a few brief moments to a world of love and language.

Whether Gilbert, Palmer, Nestor and some of the other characters in the book are real or imaginary is for you, the reader, to decide[1]. Their names will not always be found in any contemporary documents or official records, neither do some of the dates and times correlate to actual events. But it does not mean they didn't exist, or that their lives and experiences are not based on real people and facts.

In translating his original manuscript, his daughter Danielle has performed a magnificent task in capturing her father's beautiful prose. In editing his story, I have endeavoured to maintain the integrity and honesty of the original text and add further insight and context where it will add to the reader's understanding and appreciation of Maurice's experiences. The book is launched to coincide with the 100th anniversary of his birth and I hope between us we have done justice to Maurice's words.

Sean Feast

Sarratt. June 2020.

---

[1] *It should be noted that 'Palmer' is not Squadron Leader Bob Palmer VC, DFC of 109 Squadron nor were there any 'Palmers' serving with 103 Squadron at that time. The name is almost certainly fictitious.*

Chapter One - The Call

Some airmen must have been even more awkward than I was, but I never met any. My hands are so clumsy that I have always refused to drive a car, but still, on the 17th June 1940, my mind was made up: I was determined to join the Royal Air Force.

Strangely enough, it was not after hearing the speeches of De Gaulle that I decided to go to war, but after hearing Maréchal Pétain himself. During the sad, dragging months which followed the invasion of France, my family, like so many others, prayed that France would hit back but despite all our prayers, nothing happened.

We were outside on the verandah, talking about the war as usual when a heart-rending cry from my mother made us rush to the radio set. With a voice which sounded as if it came from beyond the grave, Petain whined: "It is with a heavy heart that I am telling you today that fighting must stop!" We could not believe our ears.

To us, Pétain and Verdun [2] should have been written with a hyphen, as if they were one word. Now that same man was begging his country to pull down its pants! We felt as if the victorious Marne battle was being ripped away from France and Verdun denied. He was asking his fellow citizens to settle down comfortably in defeat before they had even properly started to fight.

I was deeply shocked by that speech and felt a furious urge for revenge. Whereas he may have been speaking for his generation, he certainly wasn't speaking for mine. As far as I was concerned, the war started there and then. Petain's speech, however, merely confirmed a grim foreboding which had been nagging at us for some time. We hardly ever listened to Radio-Paris, partly because of the poor reception but mostly because we refused to believe that the words we heard were being uttered by the people of France.

---

[2] *The Battle of Verdun was fought from 21st February to 18th December 1916. The German 5th Army attacked the defences of the Fortified Region of Verdun-sur-Meuse in north-east France and the French Second Army on the right bank of the Meuse. That battle, which lasted for 303 days, became the longest and one of the most costly and deadly battles in human history. Recent surveys estimate the number of casualties at well over a million.*

Dad and his brothers.

London sounded different, and even more so when Churchill took the lead. Thanks to the powerful transmitters the BBC had directed towards Africa, we were able to hear his leonine roars, as clearly, as if he was standing amongst us. In contrast, Giraudoux, the Minister of Information who was responsible for French communications, did not carry any weight at all. Of course, he had much better manners than Hitler, but good manners alone cannot win a war.

While the rabid speeches of the Fuhrer electrified his people, Giraudoux sounded as if he was about to go reaping lilies for a funeral. Indeed, this was not the right way to address the military, and those speeches would never drive men to go to war.

Movies with images of French soldiers, made me worry even more. How on earth would those poor guys- wrapped up in heavy coats and loaded like donkeys (with outdated equipment from the first world war) – be able to attack the young greedy wolves of the Wehrmacht? When they faced the cameras, their eyes were so dull that they looked trapped in a cave. They seemed barely good enough to be entrenched in the 'Ligne Maginot,'[3] with bottles, just heaps of empty bottles of booze all around.

A sign of those times had been those French commentators, who kept boasting about their army's efficiency, saying that this time there would be none of the

---

[3] *The Maginot Line – named after the French Minister of War Andre Maginot – was a line of concrete fortifications, obstacles, and weapon installations installed by the French on a line following her frontiers with Switzerland, Germany, and Luxembourg to discourage invasion from Germany. The line did not extend to the English Channel because Belgium was neutral. In the event, the Germans effectively bypassed the Line by advancing through the Ardennes.*

10

childish enthusiasm of 1914, no songs and no flowers at the tip of the soldiers' guns.

I howled back at the radio: *"Traitor! Coward! Victory will never go to bed with a joyless army!"* How can one distinguish between a troop with no music and a herd of cattle? One division charging to the tune of La Marseillaise would undoubtedly do better than twenty defeatist divisions. Deep down, some inborn instinct was telling me that a soldier who wants to win should start by decorating his rifle with flowers. For its baptism, how would a rifle fare without flowers?

While listening to that cretin, I thought for one second: *"We are doomed!"*

***

As from the 17th June 1940, all we could do was to hope that a patriotic 'Call' would come. We prayed that from every part of France, Africa, and the British Empire, soldiers would rise. Airmen would go to England or Algeria, and the Navy would hopefully hear the call of the Sea. In a last burst of pride, the army itself would hold the fort in Brittany until enough men were able to cross the Channel to continue the fight. Shame could not have the last word.

My mother prayed all the time, while my father, letting go of his usual sternness, endlessly repeated: *"The dimension of war has changed, but its nature is still the same."*

He did not trust politicians, had been cruelly disappointed by the military and only had faith in spiritual values. Sometimes, in a crucified voice, he'd fervently announce: *"Never mind, they still have Claudel and Bernanos!"*[4] or say: *"Good Friday always leads to Easter!"* With his faith, he managed to soothe our aching souls.

We were getting quite desperate when we finally heard the Call. Of course, it filled us with joy, but we did not immediately recognise the man who was addressing us.

We only knew that this new Général had been able to topple the Germans in Moncornet and Abbeville [5]during World War I.

All we could see in him, then, was a precursor of more powerful chiefs who would lead France back into the war, all the way to Victory. In many parts of

---

[4] *Famous French authors.*

[5] *French towns where battles took place in 1940 during the Battle of France.*

the Empire, Proconsuls were roaring louder than De Gaulle, and because we were so far away, we believed that Noguès[6] or Mittelhauser[7] would be in a better position to help France.

I was so hugely naïve that after our Admiral of the Fleet Darlan finally ordered his ships to sail, I dreamt that he would sink the whole Italian fleet and become the great Leader of the Redress. Traditionally my family which descended from a long line of Breton sailors believed in the supremacy of the Navy[8], but this time, however, my father brutally brought me back to the real world: *"Not Darlan! Not that midget!"*

***

Time went by, but no one else came forward. On the other hand, De Gaulle seemed to grow stronger by the day. He commanded admiration, which to me is as vital as food and water and, most importantly, he was no longer alone.

***

Then came Mers-el-Kebir![9] Churchill who feared that the Germans might capture the French fleet in Algeria, ordered his troops to sink it. He was probably right, but several ships were destroyed and over 1000 French servicemen lost their lives.

---

[6] *Charles Noguès (13th August 1876 - 20 April 1971) was a French general. During WW2 he served as Commander-in-Chief in French North Africa. Although he was appalled by the news that France wanted to surrender peacefully to Germany, he did not support De Gaulle's urge to carry on fighting and finally accepted the armistice on 22 June, partly (or so he claimed) because Admiral Francois Darlan would not lend him the French fleet to keep fighting.*

[7] *General Eugene Desire Mittelhauser (1873 to 1949) was a French general who was the Commander in Chief of the Czech Army in 1920.*

[8] *The first Rault who came to Mauritius from Britanny had served in Napoleon Bonaparte's Navy.*

[9] *On 3rd July 1940, at Mers-el-Kébir in French Algeria, the British Navy bombarded the French fleet, as part of its strategy to deny the Germans a future weapon of war. The raid resulted in the deaths of 1,297 French servicemen, the sinking of a battleship and the damaging of five other ships.*

At first, the French felt as if poison was being poured into their wounds but after the incredibly courageous speech delivered by the Général on the 8th July 1940, the Gaullist spirit shot through the roof.

The Général - being who he was - looked and sounded natural, almost aloof. In my eyes, he seemed virtually superhuman! Where on earth did he find the strength to stifle down his frustration and grief and urge that France and Britain should continue fighting side by side? Nobody knows.

Destiny was throwing a fresh challenge at a man who had already suffered so much that his soul had learnt to subdue torture. Later, when learning about the Général's life, I told myself that it must have been by the cradle of his daughter Anne,[10] who was so sick, that this proud, arrogant man had known despair and learned to overcome it. That implacable battle against a family tragedy had nourished in him and given him the providential resources he now needed to assume and face a national disaster.

At the time I did not know from where his greatness came from, but on the 8th July 1940,[11] my wonder knew no limits: I became a Gaullist forever.

---

[10] *Anne de Gaulle was the youngest daughter of the General de Gaulle who was born with Downs Syndrome. De Gaulle's relatives all testified that the General, who was normally undemonstrative in his affections for his family, was more open and extroverted with Anne. He would entertain her with songs, dances, and pantomimes. She died of pneumonia on 6th February 1948 at the age of 20. When she died, her father said: 'Now, she's like the others.' ('Maintenant, elle est comme les autres.')*

[11] *On 8th July 1940, after Mers-e-Kebir, De Gaulle gave a speech which was broadcast to the French people. Although he called the attack a 'hateful tragedy' filling all French people with grief and anger, he argued that the risk of the French warships being captured by the Germans constituted a serious risk and therefore had no hesitation in saying that they were better destroyed ('Je le dis sans ambages, il vaut mieux qu'ils aient été détruits.'). He further warned the French people not to let their understandable feelings of outrage drive a wedge between Britain and France.*

Chapter Two – Joining Up

Listening to the radio, I could not wait to join my brother Raymond, who had volunteered in the early days of the war. After getting entangled in the great debacle of Dunkirk, he managed to reach England with just his rifle, two tins of corned beef and a scorching desire to get back at the enemy. In the event it took him four years, hitting back with the 6th Airborne Division, in the very first hours of the Normandy Landings and in the subsequent crossing of the Rhine.

Raymond's military career was crowned by a most unexpected feat for a young officer from the British colonies: Participating in the Liberation of a European capital city! Raymond belonged to one of the British paratrooper battalions to whom the SS surrendered in Copenhagen.

***

Part of the contradiction of the war was to immediately send those into combat who would have gladly stayed behind at home while putting a series of barriers in front of the men who were most eager to fight. I learnt, at my expense, that between Mauritius and the RAF, there was an almost unbridgeable abyss. Although I wanted to enroll as quickly as possible, wherever I turned I was told in no uncertain terms that England could very well win the war without me. That was most certainly true, but I was not prepared to give up that easily.

After almost two years of mishaps, I was able to make it as far as Durban aboard a cargo ship. From South Africa, I embarked on the SS *Nieuw Amsterdam* - a fine Dutch liner sailing under the British flag – and at long last, I was on my way to England[12].

It was only when the ship rounded the Cape of Good Hope that I wondered: "What will I be doing in England?" Until then, I had blindly followed 'instructions' without really knowing where they came from. Watching the wake left by the ship's propellers gave me cause to reflect.

The prestige of the Royal Air Force undoubtedly attracted me. In the midst of a global catastrophe, I saw the RAF as a new Order of Chivalry set up to save the honour of humanity. But I also had other motives.

---

[12] *The 'New Amsterdam' spent the duration of the war as a troop ship and by the end of hostilities had transported more than 350,000 servicemen and women.*

One can ignore the official reasons I gave at the time. I knew that the Air Force could kill much faster than Medicine (which I had started to study) but I wanted to have a closer look at the war. I needed to test myself at the Front without the comfort of a safety net.

I wanted to add to my life experiences, even if that meant being cut off in my prime. In my view, experience to be gained in war would be an essential part of my growing up. But why should I now feel ashamed to confess that what drove me to war was France? I felt a sense of guilt to be quietly reading Corneille or Péguy while 'Fritz' was goose-stepping up and down the Champs-Elysées. I wanted to 'do my bit' in liberating the souls of Claudel and Valéry.[13]

Just like my ancestors before me, whenever the fate of France is concerned, I become blinded by stupidity. I became a donkey. An ass. In those days I found it very difficult to chat freely and openly with a Frenchman, and I am sad to say that forty years later, things have not improved. France is the only country where I never made a real friend but I, fortunately, found solace in the splendor of its monuments. If my eyes did not get blurred whenever I look in her direction, I would say that what I then called 'France' was nothing more than an Epinal print,[14] very remote from reality.

***

Being a descendant of migrants and potentially stateless, I feel at ease anywhere. I feel as good in Winnipeg as I do in Hong Kong, Bombay, Athens, and even in England. I should say: even more in England! Like the Dupondts of Tintin! At first, I felt isolated, but England allowed me to build fantastic relationships.

I was happy to see that there was more to England than just those bulk-loads of greedy civil-servants which she used to export to Mauritius, before its Independence. She was a fantastic country and a place of noble traditions, mysteriously but carefully handed over from King Arthur right down to the Royal Air Force.

---

[13] *French authors and poets*

[14] *Épinal prints were prints on popular subjects rendered in bright sharp colours, sold in France in the 19th century. They owe their name to the fact that the first publisher of such images — Jean-Charles Pellerin — having been born in Épinal, named the printing house he founded in 1796,* Imagerie d'Épinal.

One of the bards of those traditions, Patmore[15] invited us not to deny in the darkness, the things we dreamt about in the sunlight.

Although she now seems populated with too many politicians and customs officers, I shall proclaim that I knew, in the '40s, an extremely brave and cordial England. Wherever I stayed, a face always brightened as I walked in.

But I cannot deny the truth. Deep inside, something more profound than my will and my senses commanded me, at the outset, to become, beneath my English uniform, an anonymous soldier of 'La France Libre.'

So I did my very best to save the French in me. To me, France would lose an irreplaceable degree of truth and beauty if it were to remain passive in that cosmic battle.

The future required enough French people to stand up and fight for their country. Naively, I dreamt that after having fathomed the abyss and hit rock bottom, France would liberate itself from its cruel unlawful occupiers, and most of all from her private demons.

I hoped that she would again rise high into the azure skies. I then wrote down on all my notebooks the cry of D'Annunzio[16]: *'Be blessed world of love, ablaze below the cross.'* I could not accept a world without France. It would have been far too lonely. Did this urge to help a great nation, so badly humiliated, prevent me, at the time, from understanding that my real homeland was Mauritius? When I come to think about it, I realise that I was not in love with France, but rather with its culture, an imaginary nation where I had my roots.

***

The most vivid memories that I have kept of that voyage to England were those gargantuan meals served to us on board the *New Holland*. On a tiny islet of opulence, we sailed towards a starving Europe. One night, however, as we neared the 50th parallel[17], War reminded us of its existence. Around 4.00am we

---

[15] *Coventry Patmore, a Victorian poet and critic born in London around 1823*

[16] *General Gabriele D'Annunzio, Prince of Montenevoso and Duke of Gallese, was an Italian writer, poet, journalist.*

[17] *The 50th parallel north is a circle of latitude that is 50 degrees north of the Earth's equatorial plane. It crosses Europe, Asia, the Pacific Ocean, North America.*

were kicked out of bed by alarm bells. Our ship was attacked, and the crew made us assemble on the main deck.

The panic in the air was so dense that it could have been cut with a knife. Ignorance and fear were breeding contradictory rumours. *'It's a German cruiser!' – 'No, it's a submarine' – 'Not at all, it's a Kondor, an enemy four-engine aircraft built for attacking ships!'*

Would my whole carcass start shaking with my first experience of war? In anticipation, I urged the rebel in me to take over and was pleasantly surprised by feeling instantly at ease. My mind was sufficiently lucid to see, amongst my fellow passengers, those who would get cold feet, and those who would resist, if our ship was hit. My nerves and muscles remembered my Latin courses and Virgil's teaching that it is more natural for a man to rush forward than to dive for cover. I was suddenly curious to see the outcome of that challenging incident.

My belief that I would be riding a gallant steed into combat was most unrealistic. Standing on the deck, amongst women and children, and not being hit by any bullets, made danger too remote to feel real. That incident did not even look like a dress rehearsal!

My desire to become an airman was so strong that I rejected the idea of being killed anywhere other than in enemy skies. I could not die in the Atlantic Ocean. No, it had to be Germany. The torpedoes fired that night could not have hit me as my expectations had already propelled me far beyond their reach.

***

Later in life, I had to undergo much harder ordeals, and it was only after the cold gusts of Death started breathing down my neck that I really learnt to live with fear. On the other hand, I was slowly becoming acquainted with the mask that Death would always wear, every time she came flirting with me. In the steerage of the ship, just as in an aircraft cockpit, I knew that I would be confined in an enclosed place when she would finally choose to send me her assassins.

At over 60-years of age, when through the lens of my virtual camera I look at myself forty years back, what I see, is an utterly ridiculous teenager. Nothing is missing, and I even have the jerky gait which old news reels lent to the soldiers of World War I. I just hope that it is the camera which squints.

I am fond of Don Quixote; more, I admire him! So why should I deny having an amused soft spot for the youngster I once was.

Chapter Three - The Volunteer

I am a patriot of the universe. I really believe that my planet was created for me. I always marvel at her inexhaustible beauty. However, when recalling that voyage something strikes me: to avoid the submarines, the *New Holland* had to make a broad curve towards Iceland before sailing back to Liverpool. The closer we got to the Arctic, the more lasting and sumptuous were the sunsets. Unfortunately, in those days I did not really focus on their splendour because my mind was always wandering somewhere, ahead of the ship.

Having paid so little attention to their unique enchantment fills me with remorse. But my sunsets are not resentful and, four decades later, they allow me to replay in my memory, the magnificent display I then missed. In fact, my sunsets have aged far better than me, and today they seem even more glorious.

***

The trip on the train, from Liverpool to London, felt like sleepwalking. At 10.00 pm, there was still daylight, but the whole town looked as if it was already sinking into the imminent black-out. However, that did not affect me. All I could think about was how to reach the recruiting office of the RAF as quickly as possible.

The first person who interviewed me, to check if I was fit for service, was a woman; she was dazzling, and I thought that she should be running for Miss World instead.

Apparently, the men she had dealt with, before me, were still under her charm. She was now trying to bewitch me, with a simulated naïve look that one can only master after years of diligent practice. Was this a trick the RAF used to seduce its candidates? By the time she finished, I felt ready to defy a whole squadron of Messerschmitt with a Tiger Moth. She had made me a little dizzy, and I found it hard to walk straight again.

I subsequently learnt, through an indiscretion, that she had noted on top of my file: *'Too fiery. Handle with care.'* She had realised that my passion was for the Air Force and not really for her.

The following day I had to undergo several tests. I was in excellent physical condition and mathematics was a kid's game to me. Catastrophe struck when I entered the flight simulator. The instructor finally lost track of the number of times I managed to 'crash the plane.'

I nonetheless believe that I was the first man who succeeded in placing the training room apparatus, on what would have been - in real life - an extraterrestrial orbit! The Recruiting Commission summoned me, and the Chairman said: *"Sorry, I don't see you as a pilot. You might, however, make it as a Navigator."* When I replied that I shared his views, he said: *"Good! Welcome to the RAF!*

That's how I became part of that most bizarre but endearing species – the RAF at war.

As I still obsessively wanted to be part of 'La France Libre', I pretended that my English was inadequate and managed to get myself transferred to a French unit. However, three weeks later the RAF claimed me back.

Although the sight of the uniform of the Forces Aeriennes Francaises Libres still makes my heart flutter, I was soon captivated by the friendliness and gentleness of the RAF people. I really cannot remember how many times I abused the patience of my superiors and even more of my friends. Although I must have been unendurable on far too many occasions, I was always tolerated and, what's more important, often forgiven.

Our leaders expounded the tradition inherited from Nelson which was to ignore minor indiscretions or actions. Even when they could not help noticing blunders, it was almost as if they were asking us: 'Please give us a chance not to punish you!'

I was threatened with disciplinary measures on two occasions but did find, in my judges, the friendliest of advocates.

***

Two events, one at the beginning and one towards the end of my service are good examples of the 'bonhomie' which then prevailed.

After a few days at the holding depot, my unit was transferred from London to Ludlow. We looked like a herd of mules, heavily loaded with mostly useless stuff, such as gas masks and hot water bottles. Dressed as if we were about to cross Siberia.

To make matters worse, the handle of an old suitcase, which I had packed with books, gave way just as we were leaving. Seeing that I would need at least three hands to bring my luggage to our destination, the officer took my other suitcase and walking in step with me, carried it right to the train station.

My comrades were hissing things like: *"Bloody snob, isn't a captain good enough to carry your bags?"* or *"Say, Milord, what tip should one give to an officer?"* But he pretended not to hear them.

When the second incident happened, the war was just over. Every morning, we would assemble to receive the orders of the day. The Wing Commander would call the name of each pilot and his crew would stand to attention and shout: *"Sir!"*

One day, our whole crew failed to wake up in time. A little ahead of the others, I rushed to the meeting point just as the WingCo called *"Flying Officer Ross-Myring!"* That was my pilot's name! Clicking my heels, I uttered a loud *"Sir!"* But it was not easy for one man alone to make as much noise as seven.

Wing Commander Stafford Coulson was CO of 582 Sqn during Maurice's time with the unit.

The WingCo noticed that something was wrong and asked: *"Are you all here?"* I replied: *"Yes sir, all except six."* He hesitated but finally decided to laugh and said: *"Then, please convey their timetables to those who are absent."*

There was no sanction whatsoever but the next time we met he sarcastically said: *"Hey, there goes the whole Ross-Myring crew!"*[18]

***

It is generally believed that for a large military force to be more manageable, it should be normalised and standardised but, on the contrary, Bomber Command's aim was to create 100,000 originals.

The American Air Force aircraft usually flew in formation, each pilot tamely following the team leader. In the RAF every navigator was individually responsible for finding the target. God wanted it to be so. Our specialty was

---

[18] *The Commanding Officer of 582 Squadron at the time was Wing Commander Stafford Coulson, one of Bomber Command's great 'characters' and always one for a bit of fun.*

'night ops' where formation flying was inconceivable. Our chiefs were therefore bent on encouraging personal initiative.

To boost our chances of survival, we had to develop the power to invent immediate solutions to unprecedented problems. That was a real paradox, as schools do not teach originality and we all needed to create our own. I do not think that Machiavelli, at his highest degree of mischief, could have elaborated such an incredible doctrine.

We were continuously prompted to swim against the tide of discipline, and I am convinced that some secret agents did infiltrate our ranks to teach us the art of disobedience.

Of course, practical flying exercises and theoretical studies were always carried out correctly, and we never queried orders. But what else could have been the purpose of all those stupid chores we were asked to perform, if not the secret hope that we would find ways and means to avoid doing them? To men – trained to overcome terrible difficulties, the challenge was an incentive to attain higher objectives. Discipline was nonetheless enlivening as it incessantly boosted our craving for freedom.

It is in that frame of mind that we pushed to extremes the gentle art of evasion. Our three axioms were as follows: trivial things usually sorted themselves out; if they did not, there would always be a fool to sort them out for you; and by doing them yourself, you would be nothing more than a sucker.

Only a chartered accountant could keep count of how many hours I spent on not doing certain things which I had been ordered to do but considered pointless for my training. Those were not idle hours as disobedience only became illicit if you were caught. Further, avoidance required a lot of cunning and vigilance. Disobeying orders required as much energy as obedience, but it proved much funnier that way.

I was fortunate to be initiated to those manoeuvres by a 'Master of Avoidance' He was a nice Irish guy to whom his parents had given the unusual name of Joffre as he was born in December 1914. In vain! In the RAF one could find some Welshmen who were not called Taffy, and even some Scots who were not called Jock, but Irishmen in my experience were always called Paddy.

Our Paddy was a most colourful character: red cheeks, blue chin, jet black hair and eyes as green as The Emerald Isle itself. He was the kind of guy that can only be found in the peat bogs of his native land. He was cynical, yet romantic. He tried to look cruel but had the softest of voices.

Before enlisting in the RAF Paddy had served in the Indian Army. He had fought on that great north-west frontier, where cunning and bloodthirsty looters waged a war of ambush and coups, compelling the regular troops to be on constant alert. The motto of its elders was: 'If need be get killed but don't get caught.'

From those days Paddy only recalled that the world was a jungle where he was always being spied upon by an omnipresent, yet invisible enemy. The only way to defend himself was to strike first. He considered those who taught us discipline as his personal enemies and fought them with guerrilla tactics, where he brilliantly displayed his talents for 'brinkmanship.'

This is how Paddy called the fine art of knowing how far he could go before going too far! With his camouflaged insolence, he would excel at making our Warrant Officer turn crimson with rage. However, just before committing an act from which there was no retreat, he would cleverly back-peddle, and give his victim such a bright candid smile that the latter, completely taken aback, was too embarrassed to punish him.

When asked why he enjoyed tormenting those poor chaps, Paddy, who always had some well-founded excuses to justify his pleasures, would reply: *"This is how a good airman learns to survive."*

At first, I believed Paddy to be an extreme anarchist, but he kept boasting about a Code of Conduct allegedly based on two great principles: obeying the Commandments, as they came from God; and violating regulations, as they came from men.

Despite his purported observance of the Ten Commandments, Paddy could sometimes turn into a subtle backslider. One day as we passed by an orchard, a young woman offered us some gorgeous apples. Surprisingly, Paddy very politely refused. As soon as she walked away, Paddy crept under the fence with the skill of a Red Indian and picked the most beautiful apples from her tree. After having gulped down three or four, he gave me some and asked: *"Don't they taste far better this way?"*

I said: *"Paddy thou shalt not steal!"*

"Steal? She gave them to us, they are ours. I am only choosing how to exercise our rights!"

One evening, I was sitting in the Mess with four or five cadets from my group when Paddy, coming back from an illicit trip to London, triumphantly burst in and invited us to have some beers. I asked for half a pint, but he looked offended and retorted:

"I'm telling you the full story so you must have a full pint! Guess what I've been up to this afternoon?"

"Who can tell? You have such a vast repertoire of mischief."

Paddy paused for effect: *"I have fined a London Bobby!"*

And he really had! Paddy had organised his 'coup' with an intricate mixture of planning and luck. After having obtained from a Police auxiliary some carbon paper, and declaration templates on official headings, he went roaming around Waterloo Station hunting for an appropriate victim.

After having spotted a somewhat naïve looking Bobby he started to follow him around without really knowing what he would do next.

He suddenly saw a golden opportunity. As the policeman crossed the road, an official car, driven at full speed, had to brake to avoid him and drove away as if it had the devil on its tail.

Apparently, with his moustache bristling and his voice vibrating with simulated indignation, Paddy yelled at the poor guy: *"What kind of behaviour is this? Do you realise what you've just done?"* As the policeman looked up, entirely bewildered, Paddy, knowing that people never check documents shown to them, waved his cadet's card under the nose of the unfortunate Bobby saying: *"RAF Security Services. You have just obstructed the car of Air Marshal Aldous Huxley!"*

At the time Huxley was almost blind and could not possibly have been mistaken for an army officer, but Paddy had deliberately used the name of the famous author to give the foolish Bobby a chance to smell a rat. He felt that otherwise, the fight would have been too unequal. The policeman seemed slightly suspicious and tried to protest, but Paddy treated him with so much disdain that he finally consented to give his personal details.

Paddy very seriously noted everything down and finally said: *"I'm keeping the original. Here are the duplicates. You need to present them at the Military Police Department within 24 hours."*

Paddy's only regret was that he had been unable to witness that scene.

Quite excited by his accomplishment, Paddy confided that his dream was to get an Air Marshal to apologise to him in public.

For that purpose, he designed some incredibly far-fetched scenarios, but the senior officers were undoubtedly more cautious than a humble PC. Nobody showed up, and Paddy's plans went to waste. To hide his disappointment, Paddy vouched that the RAF's most senior officers had built an underground city, at about 100 feet below Piccadilly, where they indulged into debauchery which would have shocked the worst perverts of all times. He then kept on mumbling that the first of those bastards who emerged would pay for the others.

Chapter Four – Canadian Adventure

One of the significant inconveniences of life in the RAF was that every four months or so, a centrifugal force would rip you from your comrades and drop you in a new place with new people with whom you had to get acquainted all over again.

Thus, not a single trainee I met at the initial Ground Training courses at Kenley, came with me to the Air Navigation School in Manitoba and only one guy whom I met there, joined me for operational training at Finningley, in Yorkshire. Similarly, my crew was the only one from Finningley to join 103 Squadron at Elsham Wolds. It felt like playing in a TV series with new actors in each episode.

As stealthily as conspirators, we boarded the *Queen Mary* to be transferred to Canada. On each trip, the valiant Queen - sailing at a speed of thirty knots and constantly zigzagging to avoid enemy submarines – would carry about 16,000 men across the Atlantic.

This time we were hoarded with 4,000 German prisoners, including General Von Arnim (Rommel's successor in Africa) and his whole staff captured in Tunisia. Through a deliberate leak, the head of the German Intelligence Services, Admiral Canaris, was deliberately informed of the precious cargo we held on board. In so doing, we hoped that he would send his submarines hunting elsewhere. One day, I was given a rifle and a bayonet and ordered to keep watch over a whole bunch of Germans, assigned to kitchen chores.

The British Chief pointed out the prisoners to me. They were doing the best they could. In fact, the Afrika Korps, recycled into Africa Cook, seemed to use whatever pride it had left, to establish a new world record for peeling potatoes.

I just cannot find words to describe the smell of cabbages stewed to feed 16,000 men! I finally discarded the few adjectives which came to my mind to protect the decency of my female readers. When the stench became too intense, I would rub my rifle under my nose to inhale the smell of cold steel instead. I must have looked quite bloodthirsty! I was still busy keeping watch over some prisoners when the vessel reached New York. Through a terrible injustice, I did not see the Statue of Liberty and the skyscrapers. Actually, I saw nothing of New York,

Portage La Prairie airfield.

as the train which was already waiting for us on the quay, took us straight to Moncton, New Brunswick.[19]

Despite severe persecution, the Acadians in New Brunswick - who were mostly of French origin - had managed to preserve their language with a determination almost as fierce as the francophones in Mauritius. They had an archaic accent which apparently sounded like that of Louis XIV. They maintained that all francophone persons should speak that way. Just imagine 'L'Avare' or 'Les Femmes Savantes' staged by an Acadian cast with an Acadian accent! What a delightful trip that would be in the 17th century. Moncton was only a marshalling yard, and our real destination was the Navigating School of Portage La Prairie, in Manitoba[20].

---

[19] *Moncton was home to 31 RAF Depot (formerly 31 Personnel Depot) and had come into being in October 1941. Although the facilities at Moncton had been developed to include a flying training establishment, the site was still little more than a holding camp, holding the men prior to their onward journey for flying training in the United States.*
[20] *Portage La Prairie is a small city in the central plains region of Manitoba, 50-miles or so to the west of Winnipeg. The RCAF station in Portage La Prairie was late in opening, so late that the Elementary Flying Training School originally earmarked for business (14 EFTS) was obliged to commence take its pupils elsewhere, at least in the*

Even on board the fast luxury trains of the Canadian National Railways, it took us four days to get there. It felt almost natural to travel like a prince, and I thoroughly enjoyed it. Fortunately for me, I can easily slip back into my old rags whenever necessary, and today I would gladly swap my official Mercedes for an old bicycle!

***

Ever since I was a kid, I have always wondered at the immenseness of the sea and today again, in my bungalow in Souillac - the southernmost tip of Mauritius - I always rejoice at the thought that between our cliffs and the Antarctic there is nothing but the Ocean. But I must admit that the voyage through Canada taught me how immense land can be. At 100km per hour, the locomotive literally gulped down the distance, but the scenery kept unwinding endlessly without any clue about when we would arrive. Our train went past lakes so long that they looked like rivers and rivers so vast that they looked like lakes.

On the fourth day, we entered the Prairie. The wheat had already been harvested and stacked in the silos. The bare soil was yearning for the snow which would enshroud and enrich it during the coming six months, preparing it for the next harvest. The countryside, as flat as the palm of my hand, showed no landmark whatsoever and, one of my companions exclaimed: *"I never thought that nothingness could take up so much space!"* A Canadian girl, slightly offended, retorted: *"Well here at least our soil can feed people!"*

Portage was a promise which had been betrayed. Seeing it as the future capital city of wheat, its founders had created in its centre, a boulevard twice as broad as the Champs Elysees. There were scarcely any buildings on either side, as the 'colons' finally settled down in Winnipeg or in Brandon.

Alongside us, another visitor had landed in Portage where it would reign for at least six months, if not longer! Snow! It fell and fell with a very American (or should I say Canadian) vigour and abundance. After a few days, the snow trucks had to start clearing the roads by shoveling the snow to the pavements. To go from our barracks to the canteen, or to the training school, we had to walk through trenches dug into walls of snow at least six feet high. *"Do you think they want to freeze us so they can eat us in case of famine?"* asked Jempson -

---

short term. In April 1941, 7 Air Observers School (7 AOS) moved in, and as the school was expanded, obliging 14 EFTS to disband and move out to make room. In keeping with other Air Observer Schools, 7 AOS was operated by civilians under contract to the RCAF. It was one of three air navigation schools operated privately by Canadian Pacific Airlines, and many of the instructors were local Bush pilots from Manitoba.

who besides being one of the fastest Englishmen in the 100 yards – was also the designated jester of our class.

***

The two great waterways of the region, the Assiniboine and the Red River - which had witnessed the incredible feats of Jesuits and trappers, sent from Quebec to heal souls and to tame forests - simply froze. Their ice caps were amazing; shiny and polished as mirrors. Throughout the winter, their meanders - clearly visible from the air provided very precious landmarks to the budding navigators that we were.

Our course began on 29th November 1943, and our training aircraft was a twin-engine Avro Anson – Annie to her intimates. Annie was yellow and don't ask me why, every time I think of her, I can sniff a yellow smell. She was a flying tortoise, hobbling along to the landing strip but she was full of good intentions and never let us down.[21]

Despite malicious gossip, Annie did not reverse when caught in moderate crosswinds. We must also discard the legend about a pilot, who, having heard on the aircraft wireless that his wife was going into labour, landed in the nearest field and stole a bicycle to reach the hospital faster. But Annie was open on all sides to very nasty winds ('vents coulis') and Jesus, she could be cold! Rumour had it that in order not to dampen our spirits, the aircraft's thermometers had been tuned to show fifteen degrees higher than the actual temperature.

To resist the Canadian winter, aggravated by altitude, we were forced to wear jackets and boots made of bear furs. As we walked towards our aircraft in that attire, we looked like real plantigrades or perhaps even more like Michelin Men!

However, once the aircraft took off, I would be mesmerized by the majesty of the wild, and snowy Empire spreading beneath our wings. Towards the south, it overflowed into the United States and in the other direction - beyond what was visible and beyond one's imagination -reached the white and lonely wilderness of Mackenzie, Alaska, Labrador, and Greenland. There it captured the frozen ocean to cross the polar icecap. Then, ignoring the ridiculous boundaries set by men, would, on the other side, peacefully invade the Siberian steppes.

---

[21] *The Avro Anson was one of the mainstay training aircraft of the RAF and RCAF, with models built under license in Canada.*

Every ten days, I would be given one day's leave which I spent in Winnipeg, my oasis in the snow. Manitoba had unlimited provisions of hydro-electricity and did not need to save power. In the white nights of Winnipeg, the light would create on every snowflake an Aria which, forty years later, still dazzles me in my dreams. It is in Winnipeg that I had the pleasure to be welcomed by a lovely couple – a Scottish doctor and his wife, a grand French lady.

The couple introduced me to a group of young French-Canadian girls; the loveliest and gentlest type of girls one could dream of. I am convinced that it's just because there were too many that I refused to fall in love. To avoid being trapped by a single star I decided to cherish the whole galaxy!

Why is it that in England also, despite being surrounded by sweet, beautiful and sometimes even chaste girls (at the time I thought the most beautiful girl in the world would be tainted if she were not a virgin) I never went further than friendship? Probably because – unknowingly - my heart was not free.

Throughout the War I was unconsciously in love with a young woman that I would only meet in 1950. Maybe, due to some inner clairvoyance, I remained loyal to my destiny of being a one-woman man. Undoubtedly, to be able to love eternally I would need a girl from my homeland.

Life creates for every man a pattern which never changes. All the significant events of my life: War, love, and death always sent me an advance notice giving me a 'Rendez-Vous' on a distant shore, only allowing me to land after challenging navigation.

Thus, Death made a booking with me on the 18th August 1976. On that day, my heart suddenly stopped beating during an indeterminate number of minutes, and my doctor said that I was clinically dead. Will I ever know, in this life, in which boat I crossed the Acheron? [22]

***

Today I still feel an exceptional tenderness for each parcel of French Canada, and most of all for St Boniface, a district of Winnipeg, east of the Red River. During the cold season in St. Boniface, temperatures often dropped to minus twenty degrees and occasionally thermometers even showed minus forty!

---

[22] *The Acheron was a river in Greece, which according ancient Greek mythology had a branch into the underworld.*

Throughout that cruel Canadian winter, I always found good friends to warm my heart. It was also in Saint Boniface that an old couple, M. and Mrs. Le Cuarguer from Brittany showed me kindness that was out of this world.

Mrs Le Cuarguer treated me like a son and shivered at the thought of the dangers I would be facing once I returned to Europe. She was a talented cook and did her best to boost my immune system by force-feeding me. Everybody knows, fresh scallops are a sovereign antidote against flak and hot Crepes Suzettes have the mysterious power to scare Messerschmitt away.

I like to think that she gave me such a taste for the good things of life, that my whole body became immune to the claws of Death.

In the First War, her husband had sustained an injury which had left him with a limp. When I told him that my great-great-grandfather suffered a similar mishap, it was enough for the old Breton to declare that we were cousins! As a kid, he had moved from Brittany to the island of Oléron. To reinforce the foundations of our 'family links,' and prove that our roots came from the same soil, he avidly looked for similarities between Oléron and Mauritius.

Through some clever questioning, he led me to admit that my country was surrounded by sea; that the waves were blue and fringed with white spray; that our oysters were incredibly tasty; that the sea breeze filled our lungs with iodine; that the bark of cliff trees tasted salty and that our sand was softer than talcum powder. Each time the comparison tallied he would happily exclaim: *"Just as in Oléron!"* So many coincidences could not be accidental. God had created twin sisters: Oléron and Mauritius.

The vagabond sister, who migrated to the Tropics, had nonetheless kept alive many family traditions from Brittany. Clearly, children from both islands would immediately recognise one another, wherever they met. Mr Le Guarguer who was small and very much shrunken with age, would often laugh about himself and proudly declare: *"I am the tiniest giant of the world."* He was really tiny but had a giant's heart.

I missed the French language so much that I spent hours browsing around all the bookshops of Winnipeg, looking for French books. They were not easy to find, and I might as well have asked for Apache or Aztec work In the Prairie, French was a dead language, but I was finally able to find two texts of Valéry: 'L'Album des Vers Anciens' and 'La Jeune Parque.' How could I resist buying a book printed on the 15th September - my birthday - where, the Editor, had noted that the current edition was 'reserved for the author and for his friends.'

To me, becoming Valéry's friend for a handful of dollars, was a golden deal! I was already fascinated by him.

The beauty of the book increased my pleasure and I re-read it so often that Jempson finally told me: *"Not again! You already know it by heart!"* In those days I had not yet read the myth of the Book-Men in Fahrenheit 451 and replied: *"In case there's a new Deluge, I want to be ready to reproduce it from memory. This will be the first thing to do when the flood retires while you, Big Chief Dry Throat, start replanting your vines."*

Our training was almost finished. The Sun, returning from the South, was crossing the Equator towards the sign of the Taurus. As intoxicating as a mysterious perfume, summer wine was in the air!

***

One day, as we were flying over the Prairie, we crossed a warm front which caused all my calculations about speed and altitude to become completely useless. I was forced to redo same over and over again and finally gave up. As I lay down on the floor of the bomber's nose to check the plane's side drift, I had the chance to witness, through the visor, the great debacle of the Canadian Winter.

Below our aircraft, yielding to the exhilarating call of Spring and palpitating in the warm breeze, the Red River was waking up from a sleep of over 100 days, or should I say 100 years? Shaking off her shroud of ice in the sunlight, she sensually rolled, under my eyes, her blue and naked back.

I knew that the Cold North would not surrender easily and that there would be counter-attacks from the snow and more freezing days. However, when the Sun would finally settle in, its warmth would spread over the Prairie like a victorious army advancing from invisible bases in the Tropics.

Water welcomed spring faster than land. The snow had not yet freed the soil. On the trees, the first buds were still huddled under their scaly coats, only revealing glimpses of their pink flesh. But winter was not the only evil spell which had so suddenly been defeated

In the joyful light bathing the Prairie, it was easier to believe that the little wing, which would be pinned to my chest in eight days, would give me the power to ride the skies[23].

My course at Portage La Prairie lasted five months and I flew almost every day and sometimes at night. I was proud to qualify with a good mark. Now the time had come for me to go back to England. I wanted my share of the enormous challenge facing the world and just thinking about it set my heart racing.

Today, all I remember of the Canadian Spring is the thrill that 'La Jeune Parque' gave[24] me then. The magic of this poem, still blesses, with eternal youth, the Spring I never really saw.

Maurice and colleague, whilst training.

You, my Canadian friends, are still in my prayers and yet I have never written to you since 1946! I will never be able to tell you how dear you were to me and that thought makes me feel horribly ungrateful.

---

[23] *The 'little wing' in this case is the half wing brevet awarded to all aircrew qualifying in their respective 'trades' (N for Navigator, B for Air Bomber, AG for Air Gunner etc).*
[24] *His logbook, in which he recorded all of his flights, was signed by the Chief Instructor, Flight Lieutenant W.J. Hawkins.*

Chapter Five - Finningley

My brain has tried to filter my memories to retain only the nicest ones. That's why this book might give the impression that in the Air Force, once you had a wing on your uniform, you became a sort of 'angel'. Indeed, we were not angels but during my whole stay with the RAF, I only met three real bastards.

I have no intention to write a violent thriller, so I'll ignore the first two and only tell you about the third one, to describe the species to which he belonged.

I had just returned from Canada with my new sergeant's ribbons when I was ordered to be the 15th 'volunteer' of our rugby team. I had never touched an oval ball before but had acceptable weight and speed. Abusing my inexperience, a Flight Lieutenant, playing for our opponents, tackled me to the ground so brutally that I almost had to be removed from the pitch.

He had done so through sheer malice, and I wanted to save my honour. Ten minutes later, in the midst of a run, I hit his solar plexus with my elbow, intensifying the blow with a sudden twist of my shoulder. He fell and had to be taken out. But he was tough and ran back hissing: *"just wait, you bastard!"*

I managed to control my fists but flung back: *"my mother was lawfully married, but I can see from your manners that you descend from a long line of cheap harlots!"*

He went scarlet and started to splutter, saying: *"I want your name and number!"*

I laughed and added, in French, two lines from 'La Chanson du Mal-Aimé' of Apollinaire which meant: *"Your mama did a wet fart, and you were born from her cholic."*

He had me summoned by the Base Commander. I was expecting to be severely reprimanded, but luckily the Flight Lieutenant made a big blunder. When he accused me of having insulted him in French, I insisted that he should repeat those French insults. Contritely, he was forced to admit that he did not know what they meant. The Commander, who believed that after a rugby match, both teams should be shaking hands, was irritated at seeing a superior officer abusing his position to sort out sports ground problems. Very dryly, he asked him: *"If you did not understand the words he spoke, how do you know they were insults?"* The stupid idiot then made an unforgivable mistake. He replied that as an English Officer, the Commander had a duty to protect his compatriots against the audacity of a foreigner. The Commander went very pale. His sense of fair-play could not have been more grossly outraged. Sounding dangerously calm he said: *"If I understand you correctly, you're asking me to punish this boy because he traveled 10,000 miles to join the RAF?"*

The Officer started stuttering, but the Commander went on: *"You are the one who does not belong here. If you wish to be transferred to the Gestapo, I'll recommend you straight away! Are you sure you want to maintain those accusations because, if you do, I'll have to report you too!"*

As the officer sheepishly replied: *"Err, I rely on your good judgment, Sir,"* the Commander looked at him sternly and said: *"OK. Interview over!"*

Pretending not to notice the Flight Lieutenant's salute, the Commander loudly said: *"Good day Sergeant!"* giving me a big smile. As the Flight Lieutenant walked away, he flicked his fingers behind his back in a rude Churchillian gesture.[25]

After coming back to England, we were sent to Harrogate, in Yorkshire, while waiting to be sent to an Operational Training Unit (OTU) at RAF Finningley.[26]

Was it three days or three weeks that we spent there? I just cannot remember. My memory has almost wiped out that Spa town, where old millionaires came to treat their rheumatism and cirrhosis. We had to keep ourselves busy by just killing time and to me, in those days, that was almost a crime.

In life, as in space, there are black holes, and Harrogate was nothing but an almost non-existent transit post between Portage and Finningley.

I still have blurred memories of a luxury hotel, converted into a giant beehive where every cell was filled up with a bevy of airmen. Like baby butterflies, we were still bewildered by our new 'wings' and it is true that, whenever a pretty girl went by, we would puff out our chests to show her that freshly grown attire.

---

[25] *A V-sign made with two fingers.*
[26] *18 OTU operated from Finningley and its satellites at RAF Bircotes and Worksop. Signatures in Maurice's logbook include Squadron Leader Stephen Jolly RAFVR and Squadron Leader Nicholas Haworth-Booth, Officer Commanding 'C' Flight. Haworth-Booth was awarded the Air Force Cross.*

Fortunately, from Portage La Prairie to Finningley there was a logical pathway - Continuity! While Harrogate fades away in the fog, Finningley still glows with the tinges of a beautiful summer.

***

We were learning so many new things. While the Avro Anson of Portage could only reach a maximum altitude of 10,000 feet, the Vickers Wellingtons of Finningley flew faster and twice as high. We had to wear oxygen masks and looked like Martians.

On board the Anson, if you wanted to say something other than using sign language, you had to stick your mouth in your comrade's ear and shout. Our new aircraft had an intercom system through which the whole crew could communicate using a switch on our oxygen masks.

But there were a few disadvantages too. While the crisp cold air invading the Anson was healthy and stimulating, the Wellington, and especially the navigator's cabin, was hot and stuffy. It further had a sickening stench of must and rancid oil, made worse by the fact that it had to be hermetically closed.

Being the navigator, I was the only person on board allowed to use a lamp to enable me to see the chart and my calculations. The slightest gleam of light, filtering out of my tiny station, could betray our presence to the enemy.

Once the thick black curtain isolating me from the rest of the crew had been closed, there was nothing to remind me that we were flying. I felt as if I was performing a vaguely alchemistic task, in some mysterious hypogeum where the jolts of the aircraft felt like the tremors of an angry volcano. But I would forgive anything to my new aircraft, as on my desk sat a magical navigation system known simply as 'Gee[27].'

The Butcher – our Commander-in-Chief Sir Arthur Harris – thought he won the War, and so did Montgomery! But the latter was not serious. When asked who were the three most famous generals in History he replied: *"the other two were Napoleon and Alexander."*

Although I had the greatest admiration for the Butcher, I do not know how he would have managed without Gee. She was an enchantress, dressed up as a radar

---

27 Gee was a radio navigation system used by the Royal Air Force during World War II. It measured the time delay between radio signals to provide a 'fix' on a grid, accurate to within a few hundred yards.

apparatus. Through some special gift, she had three magic wands: three shiny beams on a screen which could measure in microseconds the relative distances between a network of transmitting stations and our aircraft.

The intervals between each pair of signals would yield a hyperbolic curve. Crossing both curves would allow me to find the latitude and longitude of our aircraft, with a certainty which always astonished the rest of the crew. Thus, while going down through a layer of thick clouds, I would casually tell the pilot: *"Within two minutes, you will see the airfield at a distance of one mile to starboard."* As the aircraft emerged from the clouds and the airfield showed up, as announced, the pilot would howl: *"I can hardly see the tip of my bloody nose, and that bloody wizard has the nerve to predict where we shall be in two minutes!"*

I fell in love with Gee, as she made navigation so much easier. She further diffused in my gloomy cubicle, a delicious and appeasing radiance. On the screen, its bright rays looked like a trio of green phosphorescent tiny ballerinas.

I will always believe that the luminous waves of light emanating from Gee simply meant: "Within the limits of my powers, I undertake to guide you safely and surely through the scattered threats of the German nights."

However, the main innovation of Finningley was not so much its innovative equipment but the quality of its human relationships. Until then, for each flight, a pilot - chosen through a method so fanciful that it seemed hazardous - would be assigned to a crew.

At Finningley, we were regrouped into designated crews which, in principle, would no longer be modified.

The crew of a Wellington consisted of a pilot, a navigator, a bomb aimer, a wireless operator and two gunners. Later on, when we started flying the Lancaster, a seventh member was added, in the person of a flight engineer, also acting as co-pilot[28].

---

[28] *Many flight engineers later in the war had indeed trained as pilots, but such was the surfeit of captains that they took on the flight engineer's duties. The first flight engineers, introduced with the arrival of the first four-engined bombers, were often experienced groundcrew converted to aircrew. Many had started as Apprentices at RAF Halton.*

The romantic image I had of a crew failed to materialise. Encountering identical perils did not always make us very close. We had very different temperaments and did not feel the need to see a lot of one another, once we returned to base.

Of course, I had some outstanding moments with Eddie, our rear gunner, but my attitude was too often that of a naturalist observing some funny and astonishing new form of life. With Bill, our pilot, things could have been different. He was a good musician, cultured and sensitive but probably too sensitive.

If your imagination is too fiery to be tempered, you cannot wage war in the sky unless you agree to come down to earth. Bill was unable to do so. He became so obsessed by the multiple visions of death swirling before his eyes that he finally broke down. It was hard for me to watch nervous twitches gradually invading his face and the strange contraction which blurred his left eye making it shrink. As if it needed to reject visions too horrendous to bear.

I wanted to help Bill, but it is difficult to rescue a man who has already given up. When he finally confessed that he could no longer fly, King's Regulations demanded that he be downgraded.

I wonder what became of him after he was stripped of those wings which had made him so proud. By sacrificing his honour, as a pilot, he undoubtedly saved our lives. On at least three occasions, had Bill been at the controls, we would probably have died.[29]

The pilot who replaced him, John Ross-Myring, better known as Johnnie, was made of another metal. He had a massive head and neck and the strength of a bull, but his reactions were as fast as a cheetah's!

Before leaving us, Bill, who probably felt a bit jealous, told me that Johnnie's skull was so impenetrable that he could not even hear music! Perhaps it was, but thankfully it was impenetrable to other things too, including pieces of shrapnel but that's another story.

---

[29] *Aircrew were all volunteers, but those who found themselves unable to cope were declared 'Lacking in Moral Fibre' (LMF) and stripped of their flying rank and badges. They often spent the rest of the war in some grim backwater, cleaning latrines or other such demeaning tasks as social outcasts. Today they would have been treated with more compassion.*

At first, I thought that Johnnie was not as likable as Bill, but he was fierce and loyal. Quietly, we became united by strong bonds of friendship, based on the certainty that we could rely upon each another unquestioningly.

This trust became unwavering after what was to happen at Leverkusen. After that incident, we realised that it was risky to rely on anyone too much.[30]

***

It seems almost abnormal that the exceptional lifestyle of Finningley failed to create closer ties amongst the airmen based there. Strangely enough, it was not in my crew that I made the most friends but rather in a group, which should have been christened: 'The Navigators' Initiating Society.'

That phenomenon which manifested itself almost everywhere in the Air Force was definitely present at Finningley: Navigators often formed a very private circle, where only fellow navigators were admitted. In general, Navigators were well read, shared many common interests, and needed to be on the same wavelength. But that was not the main reason. What really brought us together was the incongruous nature of our job. When we were on ops, all the other crew members would be looking out for approaching enemies. Only we navigators waged war sitting in front of a mirror.

Imprisoned behind our black curtains, the only thing we saw, whenever our aircraft were being shot at, was our own reflection on the radar screens. Straight view in Gee and side view in 'Y'. Later on, when I joined the Pathfinders, a supreme refinement was added - LORAN - where we could also enjoy a rearview of our necks[31].

---

[30] *Johnnie Ross Myring survived a bad crash at 28 OTU back in February 1944 when the Wellington he was flying suffered an engine failure, crashed and was written off. He was on a cross-country exercise with what would have been his first operational crew when disaster struck. Jack Morley, the wireless operator, writing about the event many years afterwards, claimed that Johnnie had overshot an attempted landing and in trying to go around again had lost power in one of the engines in the turn and more or less fallen out of the sky. At least one of the crew refused to fly with him again. Johnnie's first crew went on to complete a tour with 101 Squadron. Johnnie, as we know, was obliged to start with another crew at another OTU.*
[31] *'Y' was H2S, a ground scanning radar that gave navigators a visual representation of the terrain below. LORAN was a hyperbolic radio navigation system similar to Gee but operating at lower frequencies and with greater range.*

I thus flew through flak belts surrounded by reflections of my own face. Even when times got really rough, all I could see was nothing but myself and since then, all the perils I have had to face, always attacked me from within.

Of course, at Finningley, we were a training unit and far from the battlefront. But our training exercises would imitate the conditions of real operations very closely. After coming back to base, it was difficult for us to emerge entirely from that dark cell where we would soon be sent to defy Death.

This created indefinable affinities amongst navigators. As if we were all keeping watch over a secret so profound, that we could never talk about it. The traditional joke of the navigators of Finningley was to compare ourselves to Samson and the Philistines:

"Eyeless in Gaza, at the mill, with slaves."

During our aerial training exercises, we were submitted to a pace of work which today would certainly provoke strikes and rebellions in the most barbarous prisons.

Every six minutes, non-stop, I had to check my instruments and record the time as well as our specific speed and altitude on a navigator's log. With the help of a calculator, I adjusted our speed with regards to altitude and tracked, on the compass, the gyro-magnetic course which I had asked the pilot to follow.

Manipulating Gee's controls allowed me to align her electronic signals which had to be frozen. After using the Vernier scale to obtain even more precise readings, I would transfer the hyperboles thus obtained to a Mercator projection[32] to determine our exact latitude and longitude. After having ascertained our bearings (i.e., the point we would have reached if we had traveled in static air, at the prescribed speed, on the prescribed course;) and linked that theoretical position to our real one (obtained thanks to Gee), I would finally get a vector corresponding to the aircraft's drift. That would enable me to confirm the precise direction and speed of the wind. At that point, I could

---

[32] *A projection of a map of the world on to a cylinder in such a way that all the parallels of latitude have the same length as the Equator, used especially for marine charts and certain climatological maps.*

anticipate where the aircraft would be six minutes later if the wind did not vary. Believe me, winds can differ much more than women do.[33]

One should never move away from the prescribed course, and always reach every turn at a predetermined time. After each set of calculations, I had to communicate to the pilot an adjusted course and speed to comply with the very rigorous norms of Bomber Command. I then had to re-do those calculations over and over again and indefinitely for every ensuing six minutes. That meant completing 13 distinct series of exercises every six minutes, and a total of between 600 to 800 such series during a typical flight. Talk about a mill!

At first, we hardly had time to breathe. A Jewish friend of mine had even divided the pages of his log sheet into twelve columns, separated by red lines, to remind him to inhale some oxygen should he forget to breathe! After a considerable amount of practice, most of us were able to nibble off a few seconds out of each exercise.

I finally managed to complete all the steps of that forced labour in just over four minutes. I did not try to go below that range, but it was probably as feasible as running sub-four-minute mile!

To support us during our flights, we would all be given one of those delicious chocolate bars which are still so popular today - the Mars Bar. The rest of the crew usually managed to enjoy their treat during the flight, but at the beginning, I had no time to even think about mine. As we boarded the Wellington on one of our first training flights, I placed my Mars Bar in a big green navigator's bag - where I usually stored away my maps and tools - with the firm intention to enjoy same later on.

On that day, 'Loopless' Finnigan, our wireless operator, who was hauling in the aircraft's antenna, stepped on my bag with his big boots, turning my chocolate into a disgusting mess. I was about to throw it away when the voracious Loopless begged me to give it to him and just gulped it down.

On the following flight, the same thing happened. This time, as Loopless tried to grab the creamy mess, I threw it down to the bottom of the bin and gave him a vicious look. The way in which he tried to avoid my eyes was, in itself, a confession. I warned him: *"Next time, I'll take yours."* I had hit a sensitive spot, and he never tried his luck again.

---

[33] *As one experienced Pathfinder navigator once said, a navigator cannot tell you where you are, but he can tell you where you've been!*

Since the War, all items of our original equipment have been profoundly modified but to me, of all our gear, the one which best stood the test of time was the incredible Mars Bar! In fact, after I finish this page, I'll treat myself to one.

As Proust[34] so rightly said: 'There is nothing like certain types of food – madeleines or chocolates - to bring back the flavour of times gone by.'

***

For our last training flight, we had to fly over the Channel. As we were flying north towards Dover, I deserted Gee to follow the contours of the map, represented using Cathode ray tubes[35] on the Y screen.

On the other shore of the ink-black sea, facing the south-eastern coast of England, looking like a pockmarked mass, another pockmarked mass came up on the port side, within the extreme range of Y - a maximum of thirty miles.

It was a little after midnight. I turned off my lamp and went to stand behind the pilot. Outside I could see the real landscape of which Y only gave me the negative image. I could see the glimmer of the waves, as even on the darkest nights, water reflects light.

Thick clouds were building up, on the continent, and although my eyes feverishly scanned the sky towards the direction indicated by Y, all I could see were darker masses drifting far beneath us. I should have gone back to my calculations, but I just could not resist that longing deep inside me.

My desires were fulfilled when suddenly, through a gap in the clouds I saw a white cliff rising towards my right, and some rare lights twinkling further away. The clouds hid all the rest. That is when I first saw France. Too bad for the rules. I had decided to allow myself a six minutes' break. I just wanted to look at Her![36]

Every time we returned to base, our instructor scrutinized our navigation logs, as if using a magnifying glass. He twitched when he saw those six blank minutes

---

[34] Proust was the author of A la Recherche du Temps Perdu.
[35] The cathode ray tube (CRT) is a vacuum tube that contains one or more electron guns and a phosphorescent screen, used to display images. It modulates, accelerates, and deflects electron beam(s) onto the screen to create the images.
[36] OTU aircraft were often used to create 'diversions' for Main Force raids and confuse German radar by flying close to the French coast or even dropping 'Nickels' (propaganda leaflets) over French towns. The also flew simulated raids towards the end of their training called 'Bullseyes'.

and yelled: *"What the hell were you doing during all that time?"* What could I have told him? It was a secret between Her and me. The instructor groaned: *"I intended to give you a five but will only give you a four instead."* Our exercises were noted on a scale of one to seven. Getting a three or less was poorly thought of. four was acceptable, five was good, and six was rare. I met only one navigator who got a seven. He had the face of a girl and broke down on his first mission.

***

We had a few alerts at Finningley, and a crew from our course did not come back[37]. Probably to get us used to the idea of Death. Eddie, our rear gunner, told me: *"The navigator decided to take a shortcut through a mountain!"* and added, threatening me with his finger: *"Now get this into your thick skull: a mountain has to be flown over. If you try to play funny by flying through or flying under, I'll kill you!"* I laughed because he had to stand up on his toes to reach my chin!

The crew of another aircraft, whose engines had broken down, had bailed out somewhere in the north of Scotland. Our problems were not as severe.

One night, Finningley completely disappeared in a thick fog, and we had to land fifty miles away at Peplow and return the next day when the weather improved. On another night, one of our left engines packed up, and we were compelled to make a forced landing at Church Broughton.

I was never anxious about the risks involved in training. Sandtoft, one of the three airfields where we had to complete our two years' training, had a terrible reputation. It was called 'Prangtoft' – translated into Fracasso or Krashpiste. Apparently, they used old crates which, even after having been well maintained by the ground crews, would still crash without warning. Those rumours did not bother me. I had an appointment with the future and could not ignore that curious feeling that I was being saved for another struggle.

At first, my guts, much more than my brain, told me that I had nothing to fear. But then the sight of devastated skies, hanging over towns spitting flak from every corner, quickly shattered my faith in a protected future. After I joined the Squadron, at Elsham Wolds, that future which had always seemed so clear and so precise to me, suddenly became hypothetical. The magic circle which had

---

[37] *At least five aircraft were lost during Maurice's time at 18 OTU between August – November 1944, with at least four men killed.*

protected me until then cracked down and snapped after the stranger - Death - walked in and threatened that my life might not last very long.

I was then forced to dismiss this feeling of invulnerability. We had completed 41 training exercises, including the seventeen night flights from Finningley and I felt I was ready to embark on a real operation and fly to Germany.

However, the RAF was not yet prepared to entrust to us its precious four-engined aeroplanes! It was not even ready to risk the funds that it had bet on our mortal skins.

We were thus sent to Blyton, where we had to do twenty-one additional flights to get accustomed to our new aircraft, the Avro Lancaster. In Bomber Command jargon Blyton was a Heavy Conversion Unit (HCU).[38] I was already a convert and still believe that the Lancaster is probably one of the greatest aeroplanes in history. It was for sure the one which dealt the most lethal blows to the German war machine.

Its prototype, the Manchester, had similar dimensions, but only two engines, and they were woefully unreliable. Maybe, out of vanity, the Lancaster – with its four Rolls Royce Merlins – would often demonstrate that it could fly, even after losing two engines.

One day, Johnnie - who enjoyed pushing our Lancaster to its extreme limits - decided to turn off the two outer engines. He then dipped the nose of the Lanc slightly and further cut off the port inner engine. The aircraft started vibrating right to the bottom of its guts as it tried to keep flying on only one engine. As its wings shuddered, uttering metallic moans, I felt that it was on the extreme edge of a spin.

Johnnie 'convinced' the aircraft to keep on flying by cleverly re-balancing the trim, the rudder bar, the elevators, and the ailerons! He would constantly cajole or insult our Lancaster, as if it were a woman and shout: *"Hold it Foxie[39], there's a good girl, hold it, you bitch!"* Although I deeply admired Johnnie's virtuosity, I did not want him to push things too far. As he asked me: *"Beautiful hey?"* I dryly replied: *"No more-unnecessary goosebumps!"*

It was in those days that a feeling, which had been nagging me ever since June 1940, reached its highest peak. I saw myself as a tacit ambassador of everything

---

[38] *1662 HCU*
[39] *The identification letter of Maurice's aircraft was F for Fox.*

French, mandated to negotiate with the English the right not to blush in their presence, and even less in the presence of their wives.

That mission was a very delicate one as British women at war (I apologise to my English, Scottish, and Irish girlfriends for grouping them all under the same umbrella) were some of the most endearing flowers ever borne by Earth. First came our auxiliaries, the WAAFs. They were of all kinds but had one thing in common: their unfailing gentleness.

'Smithie', one of my fellow navigators, who would be turned on by every girl passing his way, tried to hide his weakness by pretending to be a misogynist. He would tell those girls the most horrible things, deserving a thousand slaps, but the WAAFs just smiled as they were not the slapping type! One day we were having a drink in a pub with five or six WAAFs, when a group of young girls, dressed in brightly-coloured dresses suddenly walked in. Smithie popped up, with bulging eyes, pointed his finger at them and shouted: *"Good Lord, white women!"* Our friends just laughed.

The same was also true of our Sisters, whether they wore a uniform or not. I was so fond of those incurably original British women to whom everything human was so dear. They were not insular and, on the contrary, had an almost imperial touch. Their Empire stretched over the whole World.

What has become of you, little girl, who took my hand, once, on a country road, and without a word, walked me to your lovely little house? You told me: *"This is my home,"* then stayed on the doorsteps as I walked away, giving me such a severe but sweet gaze? You had the same bright eyes as those of the old granny who served at the Retford Station's buffet. She was at least 90-years old and had a beautiful quavering smile.

Once around midnight, I stepped down from the packed London train, completely stiff from having slept on my feet, crushed between by my backpack and the corridor's wall. I was feeling sore all over and asked the old lady for some tea to warm me up. She said: *"Do me a favour, let me offer you same."* Deep in her old eyes, I saw the soul of a joyful child and replied: *"Your smile has betrayed you; you are my guardian angel dressed up as a waitress."* Was the sound which then came out of her throat, a laugh or a sob? I still cannot tell.

Both in Yorkshire and in Lancashire, most of the ladies to whom I asked my way, would sweetly call me 'Love!' They called everybody 'Love' as it was a local habit, but their tone gave that word its full value. Every time you looked for a street, you found a soul.

Chapter Six – Into Battle

My interminable training had allowed me to grasp all the techniques to enable me to take part in a bombing operation. But was this enough? Words of Nerval and Novalis crept into my brain, warning me that I further needed to be spiritually induced before actually going on an air raid. If only I'd been a knight.

Thirty years later, I would be knighted by Queen Elizabeth II. Lords and Ladies and other Court officials from a Palace built a few centuries ago greeted me. They led me through legendary galleries, where paintings of Rubens and Vandyke had found a home which really deserved them - much more than the walls of traditional museums.

Musicians dressed up in gleaming liveries were playing solemn or joyous tunes. In the forefront - in memory of the vastest empire of the World - sentinels from the East, 'Sabres au Clair[40],' seemed to be waiting for a sign from their Queen to chop off seditious heads.

Her Majesty seemed incredibly unscathed by the roughness and vulgarity of our times, and I thought that she had probably been created for the pleasure of children and poets.

As I knelt before her, she softly touched my shoulders with the flat of her sword and, after the traditional accolade, slipped around my neck the Insignia of the Order. From close, she looks a thousand times prettier than in her photographs. Her smile shines with kindness and courage.

On that day, beauty and luxury prevailed. As if in a dream, I felt that the Queen was somehow commemorating in public what had happened years before, on a patch of asphalt, overgrown with weeds, in the midst of old barracks doomed to rust.

***

An atavistic memory, even more than my books, finally guided me to the covert place I had been looking for. Naturally, it could only be reached through a path of no-return which crumbled away, as I, foolhardily moved forward.

I needed to remove all material obstacles and chase my imaginary dragons before reaching the real snares, the invisible ones. To survive one would need

---

[40] *French expression meaning 'with swords drawn.'*

to be specially blessed. If I was to be part of the blessed few, I hoped our reward would be the vision of a beautiful girl emerging from the ocean, or even maybe a whole sea of beautiful girls. It was that vision which helped me keep my bearings during hard times, and I guess it must have been the same for many of us.

We did our final exercise with the 1662 HCU at Blyton. After flying 1,200 miles in six hours without a break, we indulged in the happy expectation of a lazy evening. But as we approached the airfield, the control tower warned us: *"Fog over Blyton, go to Elsham!"*

It had not yet been decided to which Squadron we would be sent to fill a 'gap' and, at the time, the name 'Elsham' meant nothing special to me. I, however, note that what happened to us then was on the way to Elsham. I quickly calculated a new course for our pilot.

The weather was deteriorating rapidly there were huge packs of clouds hovering terribly low. Johnnie said: *"Tonight, even the birds will go home on foot."* The worse was still to come. In that saturated atmosphere, cloud banks and fog zones were building up so quickly that very soon the whole north east of England would be drowned in a dangerous pea soup. I doubted whether we still had enough time to reach Elsham before the fog ate it up.

Through a slit, in the cottony shroud that wrapped up the countryside, we saw a piece of trustworthy looking ground just ahead; as if waiting for us, was a landing strip: *"Pilot to Navigator, I'm going for it!"* I said OK. In the dim light of the dying day, one could hardly see beyond 400 yards. As he was about to land, Johnnie swore: *"Hell, the strip is so short!"* and Mickey, the flight engineer, echoed: *"Yes, much too short!"*

A Lancaster needs a minimum of about 1,600 to 1,800 yards to be able to land. This runway was a good 600 yards short[41]. But the fighter in Johnnie immediately took over. *"Not too short for me!"* After two clever side slips, he managed to put down his wheels at the exact spot where the strip started and, like a jockey controlling a bolting horse, stopped the aircraft at the extreme end of the runway.

It was such a strange place! The control tower had not answered Johnnie's calls. We saw nothing of the usual procedures which that type of landing usually triggers in airfields. There was not a single aircraft parked there and no sign of

---

[41] *Goxhill in fact had three runways, the shortest being 1,100 yards.*

life. Johnnie exclaimed: *"Are we still on earth or has our damned navigator diverted us to that strange planet from which he comes?"*

For my own part I felt that I had been mysteriously guided to a secret landing strip, forgotten by men and time. I wondered whether, thanks to that forced landing, we had finally found the lair of the Sleeping Beauty.

The fog, refusing to clear, was violently striving to repossess the airfield. Oozing from every pore of the saturated soil, damp fumaroles, mixed with suspended raindrops, started to engulf the tower and the buildings below. The premises just disappeared, like stage décor being removed.

After five very long minutes, a small truck, driven by a young WAAF accompanied by an old Sergeant, emerged from the fog. He asked: *"What are you doing here? This airfield was closed two years ago!"* Someone replied: *"The fog has forced us to re-open it!"*

The Sergeant respectfully asked Johnnie: *"How did you manage to land a Lancaster here without crashing?"* Johnnie laughed: *"I just pretended that our aircraft was a smaller model!"*

The young WAAF stepped down from the vehicle and said: *"I've asked the cook to prepare a good hot meal for you. Please follow me."* This was so good to hear. Her face was pink in the evening light, the mist surrounded her body, and she had the most delicious Scottish accent I ever heard!

Johnnie parked the aeroplane, and we climbed into the van. *"My name is Renee,"* said the WAAF. *"Welcome to Goxhill!"*

Johnnie cooed: *"She has just invented this! We are in the middle of nowhere! This place can't have a name, and I'm sure we're no longer on earth!"*

"Then make the best of it, you fatty!" retorted Renee, who had overheard him.

The Sergeant explained that when the smaller aircraft which had been using that airfield stopped doing so, he, 12 WAAFs and eight soldiers had to stay on to keep watch over the remaining equipment. *"I think they have simply lost our file and nobody now knows that we still exist! But as long as they send us our food and pay..."*

In the monotonous and timeless life of the forlorn occupants of Goxhill, we were like heroes fallen from Heaven.

In a festive welcome gesture, the whole staff, led by the WAAFs, came running towards us and carried us to the canteen on their shoulders. All of us, except our enormous Loopless! With unbelievable goodwill, four WAAFs desperately tried to lift him, but finally gave up. They would have needed at least a small crane!

The Chef cooked his freshest eggs and his tastiest bacon, further treating us with his most excellent coffee. All those good people left on byways so far from the fighting zones could not have done enough to show their admiration. They knew that in one week, we would be tasting the real War. They were so kind and thoughtful that Eddie and Mickey started to behave as if the War had already been won! We felt almost the same. Still exhilarated by his feat, Johnnie discretely told me: *"Let's invite them all to the pub, and we'll all get drunk!"* That invitation was warmly welcomed with unanimous hurrahs.

However, a riot nearly broke out when the Goxhill personnel, pushed by Hubert, our bomb aimer, insisted that they should pay for the round. Exceptionally, making use of the prerogatives of his rank, Johnnie clamoured: *"Stop this nonsense, we are paying, and any defaulter will be court-martialed!"* So, they picked him up again carrying him triumphantly on their shoulders while the whole crowd swayed happily towards the pub.

As the fog slowly surrendered, things began to look even more unreal. It was no longer a terrible monster wriggling thousands of venomous tentacles at our faces. We could now see a little ahead, but there was still moisture on our lips.

Closer to the ground, the fog was still so dense that we could not look at our feet. Never mind, we decided to walk on air. Those walking right ahead of us would suddenly disappear into the night, and we had to call one another to regroup. We floated over an enchanted land where masks and berg masks would disappear and reappear according to a surrealist choreography. The damp soil had a unique fragrance which I can still remember. Renee and her friend Joyce took me by the arms. Walking between my two one-night friends, I felt nothing could harm me. With my body language, I more or less promised them that I would not get killed.

Renee had a tinkling laugh, but her friend just smiled shyly. She was only 22 but already a widow. Her blonde hair glowed like a torch in the dark. She was so blonde that I could not help thinking how gorgeous she would look in a black dress, but I bit my tongue. That night we had no right to overstep brotherly feelings.

Such evenings could be difficult for somebody like Hubert. So, prompted by Johnnie, the old Sergeant took him for a ride. He invited him to visit his stores, pretending that he had chronometers for sale at £. 3 each. Hubert spent that whole night working out how much profit he could make on the resale of those imaginary chronometers.

I still remember red coals joyously burning in the pub's fireplace. I had a few beers to help me emerge from my state of ecstasy as, surprisingly, alcohol cools me down.

As expected, Eddie went totally berserk after only two pints, but I was more worried for Mickey who was visibly falling deeper and deeper in love. Nobody knew with whom, and probably not even Mickey himself but with each gulp, he slid further down the slope of 'gaga love'. He also tried to grab Renee, but she gently guided him towards a chubby, motherly WAAF.

An old waiter suggested a remedy from Antiquity (referring to the time of the Royal Flying Corps![42]). After six pints of bitter, you fall in love, with twelve, you fall out of it. But Johnnie and I had retained enough common sense not to use Mickey as a guinea pig. We thought it wiser to let him pursue his amnesic lover's lamentations as he wept in the ample bosom of his comforter. Ten times he told her: *"It's my luck! I am in love but am so drunk that I just cannot remember with whom!"* Then doubting that she would be able to understand his 'delicate' frame of mind, he anxiously asked: *"You understand, do you?"* and started all over again. Eddie was so fed up that he finally yelled: *"Big nit, it is Helen that you love!"* Grateful to be put back on the right track, Mickey immediately started looking for Helen! It goes without saying that none of those WAAFs was called Helen.

The next morning, the fog cleared up completely, taking away with it the memories of a prestigious night. We were all busy planning when we would meet again, but I felt sad as I already knew it would never happen. No part of Fairyland can be visited twice but thank God, it is so vast that there will always be a part of it waiting to be discovered.

We had to fly back to Blyton. To say goodbye to Goxhill Johnnie flew at full speed over the control tower with his four engines roaring, while on the ground, friendly hands kept on waving at us for a long time.

---

[42] *The air arm of the British Army during World War 1 which merged with the Royal Naval Air Service on April 1 1918 to form the Royal Air Force.*

Chapter Seven – Elsham Wolds

For the second time, we were directed to Elsham, one of the numerous airfields scattered in the north-east of the Lincolnshire. Its real name was Elsham Wolds, but we always called it Elsham. To save time, the RAF would abridge all names containing more than two syllables.

This time it was not to seek refuge and the route leading there did not pass through Goxhill. We were being assigned to 103 Squadron, a heavy bomber squadron of 1 Group, Bomber Command. It comprised about thirty Lancaster crews, all of whom were ready to head out to attack the enemy at a moment's notice and without a moment's hesitation.

***

Sometimes they wander around, but my wartime memories usually bring me back to the same place: The Squadron. Today, my thoughts refuse to be classified in any logical or chronological order and survive in their own bubble. To pretend to remember just to give them some fictitious harmony, would not render an accurate picture.

Our missions over Germany meant imposing a savage rule to everything perpendicular to the homes of men and women. Doing so was literally hallucinating. It started from the moment our crew was listed on the Battle Order[43] and ended, on our way back, in the twilight zone from which we would eventually emerge, but not always unscathed.

Even when we were grounded, I remained involved in three different scenarios, which had nothing in common but still evolved around our missions.

What I enjoyed the most, was the time spent at the 'Zoo' where about fifteen of us became bound by real friendship, based on freedom of thought, cultural or maybe just our similar characters.

There were also the outings with my crew. We had not chosen to be together but felt solidly united in the face of Death. The need to survive imposed that we should create solid links amongst ourselves and that's what we did.

Being with Johnnie and Eddie was not only natural but highly enjoyable. I also had no problems with Loopless and Neville - the second gunner - nor with

---

[43] *The list of crews operating on a particular raid on a particular day/night.*

Mickey Marsh - the flight engineer who joined us at HCU. With Hubert, our bomb-aimer, however, things were a little harder.[44]

Once in a while, I felt the urge to disappear to yet another planet: London! There, in spite of everything, I could sometimes forget the war. Some of the moments I spent in London, almost clandestinely, found their way into magazines where I hope that no one else has read them.

Compacting those moments now would not do them justice. But, in my brain, the reefs of time have created new atolls, which give my archipelago a more jumbled, yet more faithful image of what those days meant to me. To respect reality, I have separated the events which then occurred into distinct cycles.

In the chapters which follow, 'Equinox' concerns our missions; 'By which Tortuous Pathways' is a tribute to the memory of Gilbert 'Gravitation'; and 'The Zoo' partly recalls my life with the crew.

***

The dominant feature of Elsham was the large triangle formed by its three runways[45]. The rest of the neighbourhood was as neat and empty as a blank page, but I just cannot tell how many different stories each one of us could have written there. Like an artist, waiting to colour a sketch, my memory finds it hard to embrace that place, which now seems almost translucent to me. It could have been anywhere; it was, after all, merely a base from which we would launch into the night – to disappear, temporarily or for eternity!

The landscape was reduced to three elements: the barracks shaped like tumulus, the asphalt of the runways and the grass. Unknowingly, we constituted two groups who mingled unreservedly: Those who would eventually survive and those who had already been sentenced to death.

Our lodgings were temporary and could be dismantled at any time, but we now felt so dispensable that we were entirely at ease in those removable homes. What

---

[44] *Hugh Bretherick had been groundcrew, posted to Iceland in 1941 as a Fitter. He volunteered for aircrew in 1942 and qualified as an air bomber after training in Canada. He died on 13th March 2010.*
[45] *Elsham Wolds had three runways, one of 2,000 yards, one of 1,600 yards and a third at 1,400 yards. By the end of the war it had enough hardstands to accommodate 36 aircraft.*

Wing Commander Duncan Macdonald (front row, second from left) was 103 Squadron commander during Maurice's time with the unit. On his lap is his dog, which apparently had delusions of grandeur! (David Fell)

kind of spell could have led men to this desolate place? A few scattered trees still stood against the horizon, like the last survivors of a disbanded army.

The animals had also vanished, except for the CO's wife's dog. The Wing Commander[46] and his wife were friendly and straightforward people, but their dog was a bloody snob! It would march in front of us as if parading with invisible medals pinned to its chest, but it knew it was intruding and probably felt quite awkward looking like a dog!

Like novices faced with mysteries known to experienced men only, the birds had gone into hiding. Their absence saved us the painful sight of wings, shattered in flight by a bullet or an aeroplane, or carcasses murdered by a falcon. Given the menace permanently hanging over our heads, such striking metaphors would have been too difficult to bear.

---

[46] *Wing Commander Duncan Finlayson Macdonald (34047) was the CO of 103 Squadron. Macdonald was a regular air force officer who had joined on a short service commission in 1933. A competent staff officer, 103 was his first squadron command. He later became station commander at Elsham and was Mentioned in Despatches. He retired in the rank of air commodore. It was Macdonald who signed Maurice's logbook on his posting to Pathfinder Navigation Training Unit (PFNTU).*

Spring had evidently been unable to land in Elsham as there were no flowers and no fruits. As if to apologise for the poor weather, the locals would tell us their old joke: *"Last year summer was a Tuesday!"*

Of course, there was the roar of engines, but even that rebellion never lasted too long. Except when the winds roared, silence endlessly prevailed over Elsham.

***

The 'no man's land' now started on our doorstep. Our aircraft, with its four Merlin engines, was a fantastic death-exploring machine! Inside me, fear and joy then started fighting shoulder to shoulder, until the end of the war when joy proved stronger. But what kind of joy? I must admit that it was not pure joy, and the urge to be part of the fight prevailed. Never did any conflict have a goal as clear as ours. While fighting the Nazis, I never doubted for one second that I was obeying the Archangel's orders. Avoiding that challenge would mean betraying the man that my parents had brought me up to be: a Lord without a fortune!

Having, for so long, defied perils over which I had no control, I was happy to finally face a real enemy, one with a body and a name, who would possibly allow us to hit it. When we did, it was no joke; during the war, no other aircraft had the punch of the Lancaster!

As far as fear was concerned, I did my best to ignore it. Often, I did not feel it, even over some hot spots like the German coastline, while approaching the target, or on the perilous return journey from target to base. But my fear became obsessive as soon as I saw my name on the Battle Order and would intensify during take-off. Throughout those few hours, Death would pull faces at me, nagging and provoking me. But once in flight, I tried my best to leave the Reaper behind by running faster than her. In turn, I provoked her: *"You, rampant, you are too afraid of heights!"* Gilbert had given me a valuable tip. *"There is the fear which paralyses you and the one which urges you to exceed your limits... Break the neck of the first and always remember the second is your best ally!"*

I had quickly learnt to capture surroundings hidden to my eyes, through the sheer intonations of my comrades. Johnnie calling me with a hoarse accent betrayed that an enemy fighter had dropped a luminous flare much too close. When Mickey trilled like a soprano, I knew there was flak ahead. If Eddie, lost in the rear turret moaned in a strange, painful voice *"It's freezing in here!"* it meant that a few minutes earlier he had seen the glimpse of a fighter in shadows darker than the night.

I did not always knowingly feel fear, but there was still some anguish lurking deep inside me. Otherwise, how would I explain this wave of enchantment which lifted my heart when, during return flights our formation neared friendly territory, gradually drawing us away from danger? Only the measure of my relief could express the extent of the fear which had then oppressed me.

I had read somewhere that some crews having experienced near misses, would, for a long time afterwards, feel retrospective panic. I never felt, nor noticed, similar feelings in the crews with whom I flew. As far as possible, we tried to stifle our fear and keep it at arm's length. Imagination is often full of cowardice, but a memory, and justifiably so, can pretend to have been fearless.

***

When an operation was being planned, navigators had to meet one hour ahead of the rest of the crew, to prepare the flight plans. We would assemble in the securely guarded map-room. On the far wall there was a large map, covered by a white cloth. In a dramatic gesture, the Navigation Leader would then come forward to pull down the cloth. We had christened him 'the Porter of Apocalypse.'

We would then be told about the target and shown the route we would take. If the slightest indiscretion were to betray that secret to the enemy, there would be no survivors. But Bomber Command knew what was at stake, and I believe nothing ever leaked out. Nonetheless, the more experienced members of the Squadron would immediately start measuring the risks and the chances. Depending on the situation, we would hear one of two legendary phrases; either: *"A piece of cake!"* or *"Shit luck!"* and accordingly our worries would either be slightly relieved or aggravated.

The route was never straight. It kept zigzagging to avoid known concentrations of searchlights and flak and confuse the enemy, until the very last minute, about our real destination.

If ever the Germans could guess where we were headed for, as in the disastrous Nuremberg raid in March 1944 in which we lost upwards of 100 aircraft, they would immediately assemble all their fighters across our flight path for a dreadful massacre.

The meteorological department issued weather forecasts and estimated the expected force and direction of the winds, for each leg of our journey. That was vital to us. Our average cruising speed was about 200 knots per hour, but at an altitude of 18,000 feet, the wind could vary from sixty to 120 knots.

Given the importance of that vector, one could get lost by just misreading the wind, and generally those who did get lost were rarely if ever found. Using the figures given to us, we meticulously calculated our course, for each section of the route, to be able to tell the pilot, precisely, in how many minutes we would reach the next turn. That information then had to be entered into dedicated windows of our log.

I must confess that the above procedure often proved vain. The real winds crossing our way were rarely those we expected. We were thus compelled to re-do and check our calculations all the time, to stick to the prescribed routes and schedules. We felt like Sisyphus,[47] incessantly pushing uphill huge masses of dense air, instead of his legendary rock.

Nonetheless, that preliminary work was essential. It helped us set out an order of priorities, enabling us to discern - through comparison - any gross error in calculations made during flight, while under heavy stress and fire.

After we finished, the rest of the crews would join us for the joint briefing. Small vans would then take us to our aircraft scattered on hardstands around the perimeter. With loving care, ground crew fitters, electricians and armourers would then proceed to last-minute checks of the engines and other onboard equipment of our Lancaster and patiently wait for the taking-off rituals to be completed.

I usually had a few words with the wireless op, who was my main link with the ground. Those last exchanges had to be strictly technical. But our faces spoke another language. We carried with us the good wishes and prayers of caring fellows, who would – as from that moment - start hoping, with brotherly anxiety, for our return. It was really comforting to be connected to the ground by people feeling so responsible for us.

***

The aircraft took off carrying in their belly six tons of bombs to be dropped on the target and five or six tons of fuel required for the trip.[48]

---

[47] *According to Greek Mythology, Sisyphus, founder and king of Corinth, committed a crime against the Gods for which he was condemned for eternity to roll a boulder uphill, watch it roll down and roll it up again non-stop.*
[48] *Although targets were kept secret until briefing, crews could often guess the target by the amount of fuel they were carrying, and weight and mix of bombload.*

After take-off we circled, in ascending spirals over the airfield to wait, at the prescribed altitude, for the rest of the Squadron to join up. As the aircraft bustled above the base to regroup, we could perceive the dark mass of each Lancaster, thanks to the two little fireflies flickering on the wing tips. Those lights – red to the port[49] and green to the starboard - were immediately switched off once the aircraft - had reached their prescribed heights. The Squadron then donned the cloak of darkness and stretched out to become one of the fifteen to twenty tributaries of an impetuous river, rushing furiously into Germany to ravage it.

Masked in its funnel, and hidden from outside by the black curtain, a little rheostat lamp was the only light in the cabin. That tiny lamp, which I kept moving over my maps would - thanks to its mobile arm - help me track, without respite, the progress we were making.

Every time I evoke those take-offs, I feel as if I'm diving into a sea of clouds. Some of them were welcomed such as the altostratus, which would hide us without hindrance but others provided a more equivocal cover. The nimbostratus always carried an ice threat which was a real nuisance. To get rid of the ice, we had to climb to a much higher and colder zone as, curiously enough, icing does not persist below minus eight degrees centigrade. But the worst cloud by far was the cumulonimbus, as those wispy and fibrous clouds could cause dangerous turbulence which could cause the aircraft to crash. They could topple over a four-engine Lancaster as if it were a kid's toy. Fortunately, the design of our aircraft protected them from thunder, and our Squadron never suffered any damage due to electrical storms.

The danger they carried did not stop me from being utterly fascinated by those dazzling blue and purple flashes dancing all over our wings.

***

Here my recollections again become blurred. Logically, when you travel at night in the heart of a cloud, you should see nothing else but dusty smoke swirling in the surrounding shadows. On those nights, however, it seemed to me that thousands of little things - themselves only particles of a million other little things - kept moving in there.

Who, as a child, has not dreamt of touching a cloud? It now seemed so natural that the child in me be let loose. Filaments of mist, rushing past the fuselage, were kingdoms which I yearned to discover.

---

[49] *To help crews remember it was said that red was for port (left) and port is red.*

But they drifted away even faster than in Alice's Wonderland[50] where one had to run as quickly as possible just to be able to remain on the same spot. Greedily, I wanted to catch the clouds and enjoy the Earth all in one go! But the clouds were full of crossroads which could lead anywhere or sometimes nowhere and even away from the World. What should I say about those poignant moments when our aircraft emerged from their summits, under shivering stars?

The landscape would vary depending on whether the stratus or the cumulus prevailed. With the stratus, the aircraft would fly over vast milky plains which seemed so soft that we might almost forget their perfidy. In fact, the dark shadows of our aircraft clearly reflected against their luminous background, turning us into conspicuous prey for the monsters of the night. We needed to be quick in escaping the clouds' perilous charms to find more discrete routes, closer to the stars.

Cumulus weather seemed to have been designed by a delirious Michelangelo. There were cathedrals of yoghurt higher than several Eiffel Towers; citadels erected to resist an army of giants; dungeons even more fearless than Babel and gothic castles which could comfortably house the population of a large city.

Those clouds formed a fantastic metropolis, on the frontier between dreams and nightmares which could suddenly crumble down into deadly vertigo. However, they would rise again, a little further ahead, driven by their unquenchable pride.

The magic below reflected the magic above as a capricious mirror. Sometimes, through a deep well in the clouds, we could see the ground. Each visible acre land was a moving grace in our eyes, as roaming beneath the stars had revealed to us, at last, how precious the Earth could be.

When I was a teenager, I enjoyed waking up during nights where the moon rises around two o'clock in the morning. As the moon rose, time split, opening new doors to secret alleys and imaginary labyrinths through which I would walk to enchanted places. *"You will see all this naked in Sarraz, in the palace of the mind."*

I have no special gift to guess the Invisible but have always been conscious of another Visible. Though hidden from our eyes by routine, there are gaps in that Visible which sometimes allow us to slide into a better world. From the breaks in the clouds of those days, I recall fragments of space, where the moonlight would mix its subtlest nuances to recreate 'Evermore', a bewitching land where

---

[50] *Alice in Wonderland by Lewis Carroll was one of the author's favourite books.*

all our lost toys are waiting for us, where we can conclude adventures we had forgotten and, most of all, reunite with those to whom we promised to return.

I suspect I'm wandering off the point. Where would I have found the time to see all that my memory now pretends to hold for me?

***

To be able to look outside, I needed, after a furious mental sprint, to complete one set of calculations in four minutes instead of six, to tie a bottle of oxygen to the harness of my parachute, connect my mask, switch off my lamp, pull back the black curtain and stand behind the flight engineer's seat in a few seconds.

While watching my chronometer in order not to miss the next six minutes cycle, I tried to make the most of those few stolen seconds. I avidly absorbed and stored away those visions, which, during most of the flights, were denied to navigators: small parcels of the galaxies above, and below, which the Earth allowed us to see.

Now I can no longer distinguish between what really existed and what I imagined. Maybe playing on my Y set for too long - with time measured in micro-seconds - made me more attentive to micro-variations between the real and the imaginary.

***

In those days[51], most of France - except Alsace and a few Atlantic pockets of German resistance - had already been freed. Naively, I imagined that hostile lands would not emit the same luminous pulsations as friendly ones. I was convinced that I would be able to identify German territory just through some pernicious waves emanating from there. But nature did not give a damn about our man-made disputes.

Of all those heavenly visions - vanishing almost as quickly as they appeared - maybe the most enchanting one came from a meadow in the Black Forest, at the very heart of Death's Kingdom.

Where, between dreams and reality, should I store that pale castle, flowing deep into the mirror of a lake, just over a drowning crescent moon? It lasted less than fifteen seconds, while Johnnie effected a wing glide to avoid the searchlights sweeping across our corner of the sky. I had set aside the delight that image gave me, as I feared it might destabilise me. That vision would return, years

---

[51] *The crew arrived at Elsham on 7th March 1945.*

later, to remind me that Peace is more generous than war. From our 'looting' of Germany, that image remains my most precious treasure.

***

I would have gladly dawdled on the way to delay the moment when we would unavoidably reach our objective, but that was not admissible. I warned Johnnie: *"Fifteen minutes before target!"*

Hubert went into the nose of the Lancaster to prime the bombs and guide Johnnie to the target with a series of commands while peering intently down his bombsight. Thanks to our numerous methods of diversion, the risk of being intercepted or struck just before the target, was reduced as we had already circumvented the flak zones. In our jargon, that meant that we had successfully avoided those areas where the locals are vicious. Now we really had to fly into the firewall, as all critical targets were heavily defended. No more weaving.

Masks had fallen. We knew the enemy with whom we would engage into that merciless, perhaps deadly combat. Two firing squads were flying face to face. That was naked war. All around us, the Carnival of Death paraded as the defences furiously reacted. The multi-coloured tracer rounds which, surprisingly - through some optical illusion - seemed to approach very slowly, suddenly accelerated, flashed madly past us and disappeared into the night. The light flak was busy.

On the ground, the deadly beams of the searchlights scanned the darkness in an almost mathematical ballet. One should not fly into the path of their beams: they could turn you into a firefly dazzled by its own fire, pierce closed eye-lids, light up thousands of suns in your burning pupils, and make you as helpless as a seagull blinded by headlights.

Fighters roaming above us dropped dazzling flares. We reacted: tit for tat. Fighting fire with fire. The Pathfinders went in first to drop millions of red, yellow or green candles illuminating and marking the target for those that would follow. The bombers would immediately converge towards that blaze, visible from 80 kilometers away, to drop their loads

The highest suspense would start when we were on our bombing run, flying straight and level to the target. On that course, Johnnie could no longer weave to avoid flak. He had to keep the Lancaster completely steady to enable Hubert to drop his bombs accurately and deal the Germans a knock-out blow.

Above: Lancaster control column and instrument panel. Below: A navigator at work. It is believed to be F/O Phil Ingleby of 619 Squadron, who was killed on his second tour of ops (Crown Copyright).

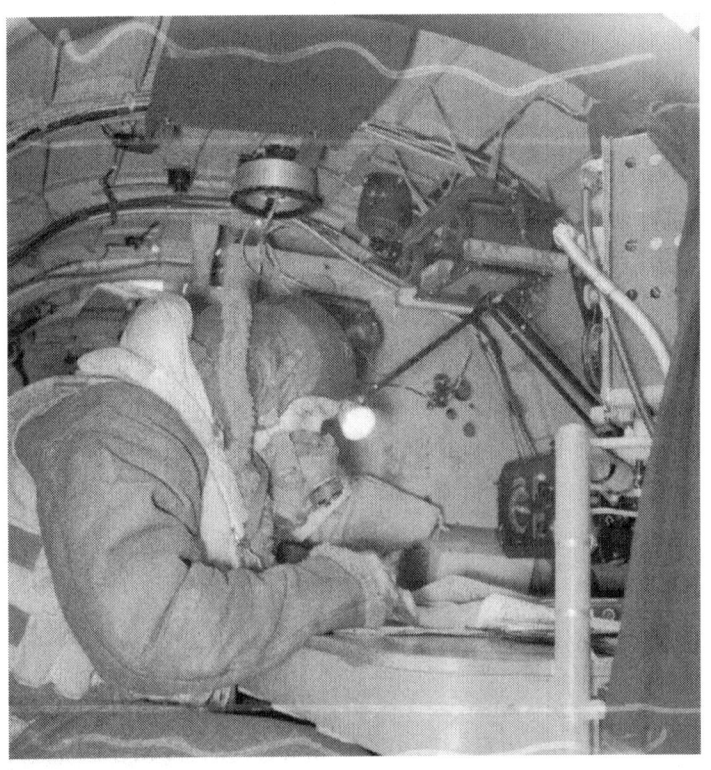

Above: Lancaster N-Nuts, 582 Squadron. (Left) A Lancaster bomb load comprising up to eighteen 500-lb general purpose bombs and one 4000-lb 'Cookie, just visible behind. This bombload was typically used for carpet bombing of tactical targets such as radar installations, V1 launch sites and concentrations of German armour.

When the bombs were finally dropped, the aircraft itself seemed to breathe a sigh of relief. With six tons gone from her belly, F-Foxie – our Lancaster – simply jolted in the air, in an ardent 'cavale'[52] while Johnnie light-heartedly threw her into a series of brutal corkscrews calculated to divert the enemy.

Hopefully, the target would consume itself in a series of explosions, like giant flowers, ablaze, in the glimmering orange light. The night swarmed with snares. Thank God, the frantic pace of my calculations sent my fears to the back of my mind.

All emotions needed to be put to one side until later and things burgeoning there would have to wait for a long time to emerge, maybe until the very end of my life.

On the way back, we always experienced mixed feelings. The first hour after the bombardment was the most dangerous. By then, the enemy knew where to find us and concentrated all its forces to bring us down. Night-fighters, mad for revenge, craved to make us pay for the blows suffered by their own people. We had killed the Germans, and they wanted to kill us. That was fair.

***

Celebration, both intimate and collective, usually started as soon the English coast came into sight. However, danger could not be excluded entirely. It sometimes happened that a German intruder would stealthily sneak in amongst us, to murder a helpless bomber which, with its undercarriage already lowered, would be unable to defend itself. Of course, we kept looking out, but subconsciously refused to believe that the risk was higher than that of being run over by a car!

Five minutes away from Elsham I would inform Johnnie that we were approaching. He would then ask the control tower: *"Can I rejoin?"*

It was always a woman who answered, with a voice as refreshing as spring water. If less than three aircraft were queuing up, she would invite us to come in, but would generally say: *"Airfield 2,000,"* which meant *"Circle over the circuit at 2,000 feet and wait for your turn"*; then a little later: *"You are number three!"* Then progressing by the minute, as the aircraft ahead landed, we became number two and finally number one! Each call, in that ritual, increased our joy. Johnnie landed our Lanc and quickly, to make room for those queuing up, taxied

---

[52] *Jumping like a bolting horse*

off to the hardstand. Those were bounded by pale blue lights, like hundreds of glow-worms winking at us.

After having spent almost eight hours crouching over my instruments and my maps, it really felt like a luxury to be able to jump down from the aircraft, stretch my body and take some long steps, while inhaling the fresh night air.

Once, at daybreak, we were returning from a raid when an incident – which I am embarrassed to narrate since it seems so farfetched – actually happened. We were flying away from Leverkusen, the hometown of Sanatogen (bloody enemy medicine!) when a flak battery, lurking in the shadows, traced us on its radars. Scientifically it aimed at us, firing just one salvo, with lethal precision.

The aircraft was about to be hit when Neville, whose vigilance had been heightened by fear, suddenly screamed: *"For Christ's sake Skipper, dive to port!"* Before he even finished the sentence, Johnnie reacted like lightning, savagely dipped the port wing. He was quick enough to prevent the aircraft from being ripped apart, but not fast enough to avoid being hit altogether. One of the shells exploded in our starboard wing, going right through it, and in a totally irrational trajectory, a loose piece of shrapnel hit Johnnie's temple. Johnnie collapsed on the control column, and the aircraft started diving madly. Mickey was shouting: *"What's wrong with you Skipper, what's wrong?"* The crew was starting to panic...

Next to me, sounding like an undertaker, Hubert said: *"We are done for!"* and, clipping on his parachute, made ready to jump. Furiously, I grabbed his shoulders, forced him to sit and howled: *"Do your jobs, you bastards. Mickey pull on the control column!"* but Mickey was in complete shock, dazed beyond any understanding.

I had no time to plug in an oxygen bottle, and in any case, we would soon be below 10,000 feet. So, I filled my lungs with air and desperately tried to reach Johnnie. But the tough one was already coming back to his senses. Instinctively he grabbed the control column and managed to pull the aircraft out of its dive. We were doing almost 400 knots, a prohibited speed where its wings could have bent. I went back to my post. In a drowsy voice, Johnnie said: *"OK guys, everything under control!"* Discipline was strict: No useless words on the intercom.

As we neared the English coast, we started to believe again. Once more, we were cruising under good stars. Nobody was mad enough to ask if we would be as lucky on our next raid. We were just content to savour the sweet and powerful feeling of being born again.

As soon as we had crossed the Channel, I could no longer control myself: *"Navigator to pilot, my apologies. I always thought your head was made of wood, but I know now it's made of steel!"* Johnnie was a man of few words. We said nothing more. However, as we stepped down from the aircraft, he raised his thumb very discretely, and I did the same. A pact was sealed between us. Each of us knew the other would be faithful.

***

An injured aircraft becomes a star once it has landed. The ground staff surrounded us, evaluating the damages it had suffered. Later on, they would fuss over a particular repair but right then, all they could think of was the danger to which their protégés had been exposed.

Our 'chiefy' - the chief mechanic - was usually a very respectful man, but those holes in the wings dispensed him from being so. Scratching his grey head, he growled: *"If I were you, I would ask myself what games your women were playing tonight!"* Later, when reconstituting the incident in our minds, we identified three incredible coincidences:

Apparently, the piece of shrapnel had been slowed down by bouncing on one of the metal armatures of the wing. In the front of the aircraft cockpit, there was a large Perspex panel - consolidated by two or three narrow vertical strips of steel - to enable the pilot to see all around. The piece of shrapnel was gallant enough to avoid the Perspex - which it would have perforated like paper - and cut right through the metal strip which only occupied one percent of the whole surface. In so doing it must have lost at least nine-tenths of its velocity.

Finally, in Johnnie's helmet, there were, just over the ears, two thick leather pads for housing the earphones. It was on one of those pads that the shrapnel finally crashed. The blow had been strong enough to knock-out our Johnnie but not of sufficient force to penetrate his skull.

Johnnie found the piece of shrapnel which had fallen near his feet. He treasured it as if it was a doll, a talisman or a lightning conductor! That bit of cast-iron had curious indentations. We showed it to the 'Rampants'[53] and said: *"Do you see this dent? It was made by Johnnie's skull!"*

---

[53] *French slang word for ground crew*

An unidentified 103 Squadron Lancaster at its dispersal. (David Fell)

Pain dissolves with time. But he who has known joy will never forget it. Any joy needs deep, profound eternity. The power of the brain to expunge from its range of perception, visions too macabre for its sanity, is really admirable.

The thrill we felt when returning from the front, made us forget that we would have to go back. Those instants were so sweet that they made the Earth look new to us. We would enjoy every single second of that happiness.

After Leverkusen, I started chasing a little round pebble, kicking it ahead of me with my fur-lined flying boots. I felt like a kid; the simple sight of that small pebble bouncing off on the asphalt filled me with pure pleasure. Like a woman's smile? A new sun rising for me? A new soul? In any case, Earth was doing its best to show me its most benevolent face.

Unfortunately, grief often darkened the bright light of our return. Almost every time, some crews did not come back. But nothing could equal the discretion of the lost ones. Many disappeared before we even got to know them, and we therefore hardly noticed that they had been replaced by newcomers.[54]

---

[54] *The squadron lost two crews on the night of March 5th/6th, three crews on the night of March 7th/8th, one crew on March 12th, another on the night of March 12th/13th, three on the night of March 16th/17th, one on the night of March 18th/19th. Eleven*

Unidentified Lancaster having suffered extensive damage. Date and location unknown, but typical of the damage a Lancaster could absorb and still make it home.

Even when we lost our comrades, they seemed, in a muted language, to forbid us from mourning: *'Later you will have the right to remember us, but time in the Squadron is not a time for grief. We bequeath you our share of joy so it can go on shining.'* In the heat of the action, we could not allow grief to distract us.

If each comrade killed had snapped one of the links tying me to the world, they would all have been broken, and the only thing then left for me to do, would have been to jump out into the void.

So, instinctively we turned away from our dead as if they carried a dangerous virus. Nonetheless, today, we are still linked to those who left through a mysterious common vow. Words that we could not speak were sometimes expressed through a glance, a smile or a gesture of the hand while we walked to our aircraft – like a promise that we would not be alone in the German night.

We sincerely believed that the Squadron was one body, from which some limbs had to be severed, to allow the others to survive. That reversibility was called collective welfare. After we came back, we would lend to one another the merit and skills which had saved us, but at the end of the day, survival was mostly due to luck.

What if we had taken a wrong crossroad, where one track leads to death and the other to nothingness?

---

crews in a single month. Most were killed though a handful either evaded capture or spent the rest of the war in a prison camp.

At the Squadron, because our reasons for living had to be safeguarded, life had become a supreme luxury. All the rest was secondary.

From the fire of the defense lines, I was, however, able to steal a spark which I managed to keep alive, and my vision changed as the world was changing. In my hands, I held a universe full of Rhymes and Reasons. Joy could no longer escape me. I had caught up with her.

Did I, while loyally following the hyperbolic curves traced on my radar maps, happen to cross the doorstep of a hyperspace? Who knows? Time can affect variable geometries, just like the wings of tomorrow's aeroplanes.

We had passed a threshold from which there might be no coming back, and now even the runway seemed metamorphosed. The true Elsham was not the one from which we flew off, but the one we re-discovered every time we returned from an operation.

Life suspended during flights, triumphantly swelled in my chest once we landed. I am sure that the best Champagne would not provide that delicious feeling of having my feet on the ground and my head still in the clouds. Alcohol, which inhibits me, would cut off this voluptuous contact with familiar things and turn into a Rampant, the winged creature that lived in me.

Walking the few yards between the canteen and my dormitory, I looked forward to something even more precious: the blissful sleep following a raid.

All the Lancasters' engines had become silent. On Earth, tuned to the rhythm of galaxies, I sunk into a quiet night, vibrating with an even more profound silence.

I then understood the reason why Elsham was so bare. It was to allow us, every time, to dress it up in glorious attire, visible only to those who admired her beauty.

Chapter Eight - Gravitation

To St. Joseph of Cupertino

"And if the face of a man next to you no longer looks alive, hold his face to the wind, even by force."

***

I met Palmer for the first time on the very day on which my crew, having at last completed its training, was posted to 103 Squadron. I must confess that I disliked him at first sight.

A truck had taken us, under the snow, to our barracks. Dragging our kit behind us, we entered a building looking like a huge half pipe and containing fourteen beds for two Lancaster crews. Seven beds were still undone with their blankets roughly rolled up as if their occupants had left in haste and would soon be back.

We had already thrown some of our luggage on the remaining beds when an air gunner walked through the door. *"These beds are already taken. If you are the newcomers, those are yours!"* he said, pointing to the beds which were unmade. I guessed the rest, but Eddie shyly asked: *"Have those guys already finished their tour?"*

The air gunner laughed and cynically replied: *"Yeah, that and all the rest – Got shot down over Krefeld! Yesterday!"* Watching our faces with nasty curiosity, he added: *"No parachutes opened. You come in just in time to fill the gap!"* It was as if the air had suddenly grown colder. Eddie said: *"What a charming welcome!"*

Fortunately, under the late navigator's pillow, I found a bag of sweets which the poor devil must have forgotten in his haste. I threw the candies into the air for my comrades to catch. The next minute, as if to provoke Fate, all of us started dancing a crazy hullabaloo around the dead navigator's bed roaring: *"Seven men on the dead man's bed, Yo, Yo, Yo and a packet of sweets!"*

The air gunner grumbled something and walked out. A little later, another five airmen stepped into our hut. The pilot smiled and introduced himself: *"Hi, boys, I'm Jack Kelly. Here is my crew!"*

Johnnie asked: *"Is the gunner who just walked out also part of your crew?"*

"Oh, Palmer! Yeah, used to be with us but he's no longer flying. Might be breaking down. If he's not careful, he might be classified as LMF."

***

Two days later, our crew was listed, for the first time, on the Battle Order. As Palmer maintained that he was still unable to fly, a reserve air gunner was assigned to Kelly' crew. He was a very young Belgian guy, who seemed uneasy at the thought of having to work with a crew whose members he had never met.[55]

I will not describe here that first bombing operation, which to us, was almost uneventful. After we returned, as I was looking for Kelly's navigator, Peter, who seemed very friendly, Hubert our bomb-aimer and always the first to hear bad news ran to me and yelled: *"Kelly's missing. To think that we shall have to share the same hut as this bastard Palmer!"*

We still felt the tension of that first raid and all we could see in Palmer was a coward and a deserter, who had allowed his comrades to die without him. Palmer, having guessed that he would be unable to put up with the atmosphere of the hut, did not show up. For a few days, he avoided us, returning dead-drunk from Scunthorpe late at night and immediately collapsing onto his bed to snore away his wine.

When we came back from our third operation, we unexpectedly caught Palmer in the hut. *"It's tough for that poor Kelly,"* Hubert said. He found it unthinkable that anyone should deliberately stop sharing perils to which he was himself exposed. In an attempt to cool us down, Palmer told us that he had been interviewed by the CO. Palmer was then informed that his file had been sent to the Air Marshal with a recommendation - based on his record - that he should be classified as LMF, stripped of his air gunner's brevet and reduced to the rank of AC2[56].

Palmer went on: *"I've asked my transfer to Transport Command,"* and as if looking for an alibi, added: *"Believe me or not, altitude makes me sick and physically incapable of acting. A transport aircraft will not fly above 10,000 feet, and I'll try to manage."*

---

[55] *No-one particularly liked to be a 'spare bod', as they were known, or to have a spare bod as part of their crew.*
[56] *Aircraftman Second Class – the lowest rank in the RAF.*

Hubert hissed without pity: *"But then at Transport Command you will meet neither flak nor fighters!"* Palmer opened his mouth to reply, but no sound came out.

**

Later that same day, the rest of my crew went to the canteen, and I found myself alone with Palmer. He obviously felt rejected by the group and wanted to secure my sympathy. He was desperately trying to connect with another expatriate who, like him, had been dragged to the Lincolnshire by the hazards of war. I reacted brutally, making it clear that although we were both foreigners, the same blood did not run in our veins. In my eyes, Palmer was just another airman, too enticed with pubs and brothels to accept the risks of the Squadron and I had hastily classified him as 'gloomy.'

Palmer, however, wanted to regain my respect and decided to play his ace. He removed a exercise book from his bag and nervously started turning the pages. After pacing the hut for a while, like a man waiting for his wife to give birth, he suddenly threw his book to me and said: *"Will you please have a look?"*

The book contained poems which, at the end of the day, could have been entitled "Odes to a Urinal!" Somewhat surprised to find an air gunner interested in poetry, I started reading. I yawned discretely as his scatological[57] style- though very 'in' at the time - was so terribly boring. Nonetheless, I immediately saw that, save for their obscene language, Palmer's poems had nothing to do with the graffiti which covered the walls of all European lavatories. In England, during the Second World War, those 'Scatos' - along with detective novels - had become the most popular form of expression.

Palmer's poems did not resemble anything I had read so far. I feverishly went through same, shaken by the novelty of the universe into which I was being pulled. I had to keep thinking about other poets, to retain some points of reference.

Some lines starting with incredible tenderness or desire rapidly exploded into venomous insults. Words taking off with sovereign liberty would suddenly disintegrate like an aircraft hit by flak. I was fascinated by Palmer's unlimited refusal to accept anything whatsoever and by the manner in which, during so

---

[57] *Scatological* refers to urine, faeces or other obscene material referred to in a movie, book or show.

many nights - heavy with blood and thunder - he had been clamouring that refusal.

I will not ponder any more on those poems, which have probably disappeared by now. On that night, however, I felt that Palmer had genius, as a poet. Reading that notebook had reversed my former opinion of Palmer entirely.

Far from helping me to understand him better, what I had learned was cladding Palmer in a bright, almost blinding mist. Most of all, I could not understand why somebody so disgusted by the lives of other men, was refusing to risk his own.

I could not help telling him so. Bizarrely - as if speaking to himself - he replied: *"I can only write this when I'm not thinking of Ann!"* and I did not ask any further questions. Strangely, on the Squadron events often seemed to accelerate and I actually met Ann that very night.

I was with Eddie, at the Old White Swan, a pub in Scunthorpe which had been renamed the Lame Duck by its regular clients. It was a popular hunting ground, to which airmen on leave and girls from the neighborhood systematically converged. No one gave a damn about who was hunting or who was being hunted! As usual, it was packed and very noisy. Standing on a table at the far end of the room, with loads of medals glittering on his chest, a senior officer was singing.

I could not make out the words, but it was clear from the number of giggles in the female audience, that his song was rather bawdy.

Followed by Eddie, I walked to the bar, opening the way with my shoulders, when a gigantic Canadian, disfigured by burns and wearing a purple hole where his nose had been - stood up right next to me and howled: *"I want Ivy!"*

Two drunk girls hanging around his neck tried to calm him down but, as if he did not notice their presence, he hauled them to the door howling louder and louder: *"I want Ivy!"*

Eddie grabbed two empty seats and whispered into my ear: *"Oh, there goes Palmer and the French Revolution! A beautiful face on top of a spike,"* and almost immediately, I saw Palmer and his tall, skinny, beautiful girlfriend rushing towards us. Palmer proudly said: *"Please meet Ann."*

Ann sat down with us. As soon as she had heard the news about Palmer, she had come up from London as, more than anything else, she wanted him to fly again. Maybe it was just an illusion, but she immediately treated me as a childhood friend and acted as if I was the first of Palmer's mates she had ever met. That familiarity irritated me at first, but soon, her narrow eyes in that delicate, almost unreal tinge of blue which bathes some of Chagall's paintings, won my sympathy. She was sensitive to omens, saw our first meeting as a good sign, and believed that I might help Palmer fight his demons.

While Palmer went to fetch our drinks, she maintained that if Fred – that was his name – could be given 15 days' leave, he would be able to relax, recover from his depression and resume fighting. I disagreed and told her that if Palmer did not immediately overcome his fears, he never would. To me, Palmer was still in that ambiguous zone where the shame in falling apart was keeping his fear in check. Once he decided to leave the Squadron, the way back would seem too harsh and too remote. Laying deep in his own trap, he would feel more comfortable to quit once and for all. *"So?"* she asked anxiously. Eddie said: *"There will surely be an important operation tomorrow and if only Palmer agreed to be part of it, I would gladly give him my place."*

"Yes Eddie, please be sick!"

Eddie howled: *"Will the two of you send me wreaths when the RAF kicks me out?!"*

Rundstedt[58] had entered the Ardennes[59], and the Butcher was furiously sending his crews into that slot to slow down the German rush to Antwerp.

I realized that we were not being very diplomatic and did not insist as Palmer was already coming back with four half-pints. I instantly felt that, through some secret alliance, Ann had enrolled me in her desperate crusade to save the man she loved. As I filled up her glass, she discretely told me: *"We need to talk. Meet me at Brigg's Inn tomorrow!"* Brigg was a small village close to the airfield. I admired the fact that, regardless of everything else, she wanted to make sure I'd be there.

Early the next day, we met at the Inn to set up our Master Plan. Ann thought that although Palmer was obsessed by all the horrors he had witnessed during his operations to Germany, she believed that he was further haunted by more obscure, almost invulnerable 'ghosts'. To fight his anguish, she was proposing the most efficient of weapons: a clear mission with precise tasks to perform. Eddie would, willy-nilly, have to simulate an indisposition, and Palmer would

---

[58] *Von* Rundstedt *was a Field Marshal in the Wehrmacht during World War II and one of Hitler's most competent military chiefs.*

[59] *The Battle of the Bulge had petered out by mid-January 1945.*

have to volunteer to replace him. The reserve air gunner would undoubtedly be thrilled!

As Eddie had earned outstanding marks during our previous operations, no one would suspect him. In any case, as long as our aircraft took off, there would be no questions asked. I laughed up my sleeve at the thought of Hubert's face! He thought Palmer brought bad luck, but this time he would have no say in matters.

Convincing Eddie seemed possible. I told Ann: *"There's one argument that Eddie just can't resist. Have you met any beautiful brunettes in Scunthorpe?"* Ann clapped her hands and added: *"Yes, my lodger's daughter Brenda; she's tailor-made for Eddie!"* That only left Palmer. After reading his poems, I knew that the slightest pressure could turn him into a hero or a reject and hesitated to provoke the reactions Ann was hoping for. I proposed to persuade Eddie first and secure his backing before approaching Palmer. But Ann had a brilliant idea: *"Eddie and Fred have very different goals. Let's tackle them together. One will surely embarrass the other!"*

We agreed that I would ask Eddie for tea at Briggs' Inn, where Ann would be waiting for us with Brenda and Palmer. He did not sense the snare and instantly made a blunder that sent him flying into our trap. Instead of hanging on to his own imaginary illness, he first refused on the grounds that it would not be fair to Eddie. However - as Ann had already whispered in my ear with profound ingratitude - Brenda did not need more than fifteen minutes to get Eddie started. While sexily unveiling her beautiful legs – which our air gunner must have found more convincing than all her other arguments - she deviously persuaded him that, by staying in bed with her, he would be performing a heroic act, allowing Palmer to fly with us to Germany. Eddie pretended to resist a little further just for the pleasure of being begged by our wily Brenda.

Palmer's defenses were deeply shaken by the defection of his treacherous ally. He needed to accept our proposal or confess that he was afraid. Remembering Palmers' strange confession: *"I can only write like this when I am not thinking of Ann,"* I realised that somehow Ann's personality undermined Palmer's courage. Deep down, I could understand. Being with her tasted like eating warm bread with milk. Her soft domesticity probably tempered Palmer's need to expel the fury and self-directed anger which suffocated him. As Palmer clammed up, I thought we had lost the battle.

By showing me the manuscript of his 'Odes to a Urinal,' Palmer had given me a dangerous weapon. I was probably the first person to have seen his work and, though I did not ask Ann, I am still convinced that she had never read his poetry.

Although he never gave the slightest hint of literary vanity, I was his only audience, and he did not want to disappoint me. While Palmer wished to provide Ann with a token of my respect and admiration, he enjoyed watching his own image in the deforming, but flattering mirror of that admiration.

I, therefore, allowed him to believe that his poetry needed to be tested and that its value would be compromised if the life of its author lost its authenticity. Faced with such blackmail, Palmer was visibly losing ground, when Brenda - trying to be funny - stupidly remarked: *"Hi Eddie, can you just imagine the CO's face when, while promenading his lantern through the airfield to find a spare gunner, he sees Fred jumping up and shouting: 'Lafayette here we are!'"* Surprisingly, Palmer started laughing and seemed to be no longer afraid: *"Ok, just to see that, I'll do it."*

Palmer loudly called out to the waitress: *"Please, bring us a case of French Champagne and some caviar,"* and, as the girl's eyes nearly popped out, he added: *"or perhaps some cheese sandwiches and five cups of tea."* The next moment turned into one of those noisy and ebullient waves of bliss - which sometimes engulfs groups of airmen between two missions. Rolling over in its wake of laughter and crazy jokes but still filled with a deep sense of urgency, we decided that night to spend all our reserves of childishness and euphoria. The five of us, together, did not even add up to a hundred years. Ann, having reached her goal, very quickly looked serious again and was lost in deep thought.

I asked Eddie to say nothing to Johnnie. After all, Palmer was an experienced gunner, and Johnnie was the kind of pilot who could fly anywhere, with anybody.

We had to be back at the airfield by 6-00pm at the latest. Ann and Brenda left for Scunthorpe, while Eddie, Palmer and I cycled all the way back. As we came in, we saw two policemen placing wire around the telephone booth. That meant, a bombing operation was imminent as all links with the outside world were being severed. Johnnie told us that the bombers would fly at 2-00 am. We were being 'locked up' for a problematic night where Ann, Brenda, and all their sisters would become distant mirages, and Brigg's Inn seem more remote than the Polar Star. The latter, however, would be watching over us. I threw myself down on my couch and immediately sank into a deep torpor, punctuated by strange dreams.

***

A few hours passed. Our four propellers, roaring at 2,650 revs per minute caused the whole aircraft to vibrate as we rushed towards Dusseldorf. The darkness was so thick that even the stars seemed to have deserted the sky. Never had an operation weighed so much on my nerves. Strange drowsiness was engulfing me, and I really had to struggle with all my limbs to shake it away.

Just using my compass or my calculator required disproportionate efforts, but what worried me most, were my maps. They were all wide open in my cramped cubicle, and nasty little gusts of wind kept blowing them up to my face, over and over again. This made breathing even harder, and the light was so faint that I could hardly see the markings and remarks noted on my flight plan.

Mechanically I flattened down the maps with the back of my hands as I desperately tried to find our route through the incredible darkness which Germany had poured into the sky to weaken the glow of my lamp. A loud 'Corkscrew, Port, Go!'[60] on the microphone brutally pulled me out of an absurd mental abyss where I was sinking and threw me back into cruel reality.

My body felt 10 times heavier than usual and was stuck to the fuselage by centrifugal forces. I realized that Johnnie had violently swerved the Lancaster to the left in a frightening corkscrew. Simultaneously, my damned maps, as if enlarged by evil spirits, became so inflated that they filled up my cubicle, blew right over my mouth and started to suffocate me. In a considerable effort, I rolled myself up into a ball, trying to offer a smaller surface to German bullets.

My flesh anticipated the first impacts of cannon, and I tried to protect my face with the metal plate of my radar. Surprisingly enough, it felt soft and warm against my cheek. Although I was sure that we were flying over Germany at the height of 25,000 feet by Latitude 58.48 degrees north and Longitude 6.24 degrees, I had, at that precise moment, not just an impression but a tangible, almost physical certainty, that I was crossing over two distinct sides of reality. I could decide to pursue my operation or wake up in my bed at Elsham.

Sometimes, even now, I involuntarily press a secret key in my brain which immediately rewinds and replays that eerie ambiguous hour. Those memories are so vivid that I still have doubts about whether they were just the illusions of

---

[60] *A corkscrew was the standard evasive manoeuvre when attacked by a night fighter but put a tremendous strain on the airframe. The series of dives and turns also demanded particular strength from the pilot.*

a sleeping man or if - during one second – a link in the time chain snapped as I entered the kingdom of forbidden liberty.

While I marveled at the soft warmth of metal against my cheek, still torn between pursuing my mission and returning to my barracks, that fragile equilibrium suddenly crumbled down. I woke up in my bed. My cheek was not against the radar screen but against my pillow!

As I lifted the sheet which covered my eyes, I saw Palmer. He was kneeling next to my bed with his head completely buried in my blankets. Palmer was clearly in the middle of a nightmare and was howling like a wounded animal: *"Corkscrew, Port, Go!"* As I jumped out of bed, Palmer did not even look up and simply mumbled: *"Sorry, I thought you were a Messerschmitt!"*

I looked at my watch. It was already 11-00pm, and in one hour, the guards would come and fetch me for the operational briefing. I took Palmer by his shoulders and violently shook him like an old rug: *"Come on Palmer, you need to sleep!"* I let go of him, but he sagged down on his bed like a broken puppet and desperately moaned: *"No, no, no..!"* By that time, all the members of our crew had woken up.

Hubert started making bitter comments about persons who should retire if they wanted to or at least allow the real fighters to rest. Eddie murmured: *"So, I guess I'm coming too!"* I merely nodded as I was afraid my voice might break. Our efforts turned out to be useless. A nightmare had been enough to crush Ann's whole combat to free Palmer from his demons.

Several weeks later, I asked for a short leave as I needed a break. I was lying down on the lawn, in St. James Park, enjoying the moist warmth of the March sun on my eyelids, when a shadow hid its light from me. I opened my eyes and saw Ann, smiling shyly. She did not beat about the bush and told me the rest of the story.

Palmer - who had been posted to Kenley, an airfield in Surrey - had not replied to any of her letters. When Ann finally decided to visit him, he took her to a pub in Croydon. He then grabbed an artificial blonde, sat her on his knees and both did their best to be utterly disgusting towards Ann. No one knew better than me, the weapons which the author of 'Odes to a Urinal' could use against her.

Suspecting that Palmer probably felt even more abandoned than she did, Ann tried to contain herself, in the hope of seeing him alone later. When the stupid blonde sheepishly said: *"Your friend does not seem in a hurry to leave, why don't you invite her to sleep with us?"* Ann could not take it anymore and ran away in tears.

The day after Ann left, as Palmer was moving backward near a Spitfire, about to take off, his right arm got caught in the propeller and was ripped off. As soon as Ann heard about the accident, she immediately went to see him. Palmer's fake blonde was already there, and each time Ann visited him, she always stood between them.

Hiding behind the skirts of that girl, Palmer was horrible to Ann, making her feel like a swallow in front of a snake. Ann, however, noticed that the blonde was incapable of being nasty for long and that she was a very competent and devoted nurse. As Ann's presence evidently revived Palmer's sexual desire for her, she finally decided to leave him for good.

After telling her story, Ann looked as lost as a soldier undergoing a debriefing after a harsh battle and remained silent for a while. I invited her for dinner, but she apologized, saying that she had to catch a train to the North. I never saw her again and never knew her surname.

I met Palmer for the last time, a few days after the war ended. I was stepping off the tube at Charing Cross when a passenger rushed in and banged into me: *"Palmer!"*

I tried my best not to look at his missing arm, but Palmer viciously shook his empty sleeve under my nose and yelled: *"So much the enemy didn't get!"* A smile, which could either be heinous or triumphant, slashed his face as he jumped onto the train quickly disappearing into the tunnel.

Chapter Nine – The Zoo

As I walked into the dormitory, Eddie shouted: *"Attention!"*

All the crew members froze, and Eddie pretended to salute most vigorously with a tremor in his hand. They wanted me to ask for an explanation, but I deliberately said nothing. Instead, I pretended to review them, with the disgusted scorn of an old adjutant, inspecting a batch of freshly recruited incompetent young men. I pointed at the tummy of Loopless Finnigan, our wireless operator, and asked: *"Do you keep your pillow under your belt or are you in an advanced stage of pregnancy?"* Then to Eddie, whose face was as red as a cockerel's comb: *"Your look is improper! Don't you know that Britons at war paint themselves in blue not in red!"*

Eddie was not at all embarrassed by my remark but immediately changed his style and century. He twirled his beret as if it was the feathered hat of a musketeer, bowed to me as if I was Louis XIII, and said: *"Will your Majesty allow his humble valet to convey a message received from the powerful and noble Lord Gilbert V...? His Excellency having been unable to contact Your Majesty, begs you to be kind enough to visit him in his modest castle, the bloody barrack 12!"* Even in the shoes of a musketeer, Eddie's sentences would have been incomplete if they did not include the word 'bloody.'

I was happy, but a little worried too. Our Squadron had an admirable tradition. To perfect his official training, every new navigator would be assigned to a veteran who would become his personal mentor. The latter would discuss each operation with his junior, try to identify any weaknesses and find possible solutions. If Gilbert V was looking for me, it probably meant that I had been assigned to him. He was renowned in the whole Squadron for exploits of extreme, if not crazy bravery against the enemy and for his unlimited impertinence towards any form of authority, be it civil or military. Rumour had it that, after deciding that stealing policemen's helmets in Oxford had become boring, he had decided to collect their belts instead! Gilbert later told me that this was pure fiction.

I would like to open a parenthesis here. Amongst the mental flexibility exercises to which we were submitted, I keep vivid memories of the 'Grope.' It was a Torture Chamber where our chronometers were confiscated and replaced by clocks programmed to show one hour after only forty minutes. Although it sounded so simple, that device was incredibly efficient. After a round in the Grope, when using regular clocks again, time seemed easier to beat, and that feeling made us stronger. The biggest hurdle for navigators was the nerve-racking speed at which - nonstop -we had to finish and check our workings. The slightest error could carry Death Penalty! If an aircraft strayed off track, it necessarily increased the risks of the whole formation popping up on the enemy's radars and being shot down. Even if the aircraft managed to escape, the navigator would still be taken to task for making such an error. I cannot say what would have been worse to me: humiliation or death?

The rhythm of our lives seemed forever in a state of crazy flux, and we really had no time to choose our comrades. Although my good sense tells me that I must have taken at least three days to make friends with Gilbert, my memory insists that it took less than fifteen minutes. As I walked into the room, my instructor came towards me saying: *"Are you, Maurice? I am Gilbert!"* Although I was only a Flight Sergeant and he was an officer, using first names was current practice in the Air Force. In the Squadron, hierarchy was different and barriers - which usually separated senior and junior officers in the Army and the Navy - did not exist.

In our eyes all those who flew were equal. I admit that the Rampants were probably a little less equal because, unlike us, they did not have the key to that private kingdom where Death could be waiting soon.

Gilbert gave me such a warm smile that I remained on my guard. He probably greeted every newcomer in the same way. However, as from our first encounter, I was ready to vouch that all the good things I had heard about that man were not exaggerated and that the wrong things were simple slander. The actual reason why he was always so gentle, was his infinite kindness. He had a most unique and personal way of teaching. Our benevolent Mentors would usually teach us practical navigation methods. Gilbert further showed me ways and means of staying on the right track, if ever our equipment packed up under enemy fire.

In his eyes, technicalities were secondary. He did not teach me tricks but style. He wanted me to react, like he would have, in any crisis situations.

Later, just to tease him, I said: *"During your bullfighting courses do you really care whether I can save my skin as long as I behave when facing the fire?"* He looked at me thoughtfully and quietly said: *"How much would one be worth without the other?"*

During my induction, he discretely tested me on other grounds too, but I did not realise that he was doing so. He was thrilled to learn that I had read his favourite poets: Hopkins, Eliot, and Auden. Nonetheless, he still secured some further references before asking me one night: *"Would you like to come with me to the Zoo?"*

The Zoo was a semi-secret society led by Gilbert. Attendance fluctuated along with the raids, but that week it included seven navigators, four pilots, two air gunners and one of our doctors.

The doctor had been admitted because he had, voluntarily, participated in several perilous missions. He wanted to assess - from close up - the behaviour of the crews he had to treat and heal, but he further had a 'flying spirit.' Before I joined the Zoo, they used to call him 'Doc,' but after I baptized him 'Toubib[61],' all the others did the same. They thought that name suited him better.

A few carefully selected WAAFs were also allowed to join us. Gilbert, who often tried to look more severe than he was (which was his way of making fun of himself) called them 'Our Honourary Members.'

Despite being a Don Juan at heart, Gilbert did not want the Zoo to turn into a brothel and once expelled a girl who was so drunk that she acted in a very vulgar way. I asked: *"Too easy to screw?"* He replied: *"No, too easy to be screwed."*

When I joined the Zoo, only two of its founder members were still alive. Those survivors were Gilbert and Edward French - who was, at the time, being treated in a specialized hospital in East-Grinstead. A team of surgeons, who had already operated on him at least ten times, was still desperately trying to graft onto his head a new face to replace the one that had burnt over the Ruhr.

***

Montherlant[62] wrote that it was all the words they never spoke that made corpses so heavy in their coffins. Yes, some of us would never have coffins, and we wanted to travel 'light.' Thus, at the Zoo, we never stopped talking. Was it to create a counter-balance that Gilbert brought along Nestor Antinestor?

Nestor was a navigator, and we gave him that nickname because he seemed so fabulously old to us. He admitted being 39-years old, but some whispered that he was at least forty-three.

---

[61] *Toubib is French slang for Doctor. The Doctor in this case is believed to be Flying Officer Robert 'Doc' Henderson who, along with the station Padre, flew their fair share of operations to understand the pressures faced by the men under their care.*
[62] *French author.*

There were two contradictory theories regarding the origins of Nestor. For the Toubib, he was the Original Nestor, depicted by Homer in the Iliad' and the 'Odyssey' [63] but Gilbert insisted that he was not 'real.' According to him, Nestor was only a propaganda device, concocted by the Butcher to confirm that old soldiers never die: *"That Butcher's rotten with tricks, but as usual, he's made a blunder! Speech was the only thing that Nestor lacked, and that betrayed the Butcher's Robot."*

The Toubib would invent the most incredible stories about Nestor insisting that age had caused him to forget the human language. In fact, unlike his Homeric homonym, Nestor never spoke, and that is why we called him 'Antinestor.' He would endlessly chew on an old pipe which he only lit once in a while. It would burn for a few minutes in a faint glow.

The Toubib explained that on the 3rd September 1939, while Nestor was buying his weekly stock of tobacco, the salesgirl announced that the war had been declared.

Apparently, Nestor - who was still talking in those days - tried to impress her and said: *"I will buy no more tobacco until Victory!"* According to the Toubib, Nestor needed to keep his word and make his pleasure last.

The Toubib, who could contradict himself without shame, further insinuated that there was a mysterious link between Nestor's stock of tobacco and the end of the war. If only Nestor could smoke the whole lot in one night, Victory would immediately be ours.

When the entire Zoo started begging Nestor to smoke, he chuckled, tapped his pipe with his lighter, allowed the flame to flicker during a second or two and die again amidst our shouts of disappointment. With a weary hand, Nestor then indicated to us that he had no power to hasten up History!

The Toubib accused Nestor of being an Impostor. He swore that in the 5th Century BC, a Thessalian witch had taught Nestor infallible tricks to stop any war but that Nestor – being an egotist and a miser - was allowing the war to drag on so he could save on tobacco!

---

[63] *In the Iliad and the Odyssey, Nestor is a very old wise man who is the transmitter of memory essential to create heroes.*

An air gunner added that he had once caught Nestor mumbling strange words and that almost immediately rain started pouring from a clear blue sky. A little later, while Nestor was being accused of performing more witchcraft, the gunner put up his finger and said: *"Who is not dumb?"* This became a tradition at the Zoo. Every time Nestor's name was pronounced, somebody had to be the first to say: *"Who is not dumb?"*

Nestor never made any comments but, one night, as the Toubib was telling us about Nestor's latest adventures in the *Atlantide*, Nestor caught us with our pants down. As soon as the Toubib said: *"Ah Nestor..."* he took his pipe out of his mouth and said: *"Who is not dumb?"* The Toubib howled: *"Oh, it speaks! It speaks! Great, everybody can have a drink - on Nestor!"*

Before the war, Nestor had been a professor of Ancient History, but we thought that was too easy an alibi. Since he could talk, he would have to tell us his true story.

***

When I first met Nestor, he was already wearing the Caterpillar Club's pin. That little gold caterpillar reminded one and all that he had jumped from a crashing aircraft, with a parachute and owed his life to the silkworm industry[64]. It had happened over occupied France, and Nestor managed to find a resistance network which helped him cross over to Spain.

On the 24th March 1945, his aircraft was shot down over Dortmund, but he again managed to jump. After an eventful journey, requiring a lot of cunning and courage, he managed to reach the American lines. [65]

A young German girl had helped him, and that confirmed one of the Toubib's theories: *"Man is the only creature who is stupid enough to be nationalist. Women, as all true animals, are stateless. They will never accept that any artificial frontiers – only existing on paper – should stop them from choosing the men they want! That is why if you are shot down over enemy territory and cannot manage on your own, contact the first woman you meet. If she likes your*

---

[64] *The Caterpillar Club was founded by the Irvin Parachute Company in Letchworth, Hertfordshire. A gold caterpillar with emerald eyes was given to any airman whose life was saved by one of their designs.*

[65] *Three aircraft were shot down on the Dortmund Raid, from 150, 166 and 550 Squadrons. From the 150 Squadron Lancaster from Hemswell, two baled out and survived. The other five, including the navigator, also made it out only to be killed after being taken into custody.*

face, she will be on your side and even more so if you don't speak her language. Incoherence is a powerful way to seduce a woman. Look at the Poles, women simply fall into their laps."

He would then, very unjustly, add: *"However, in friendly territory better go to a man as they are more discrete, especially the priests. Even those can be useful sometimes!"*

Just after the war, Nestor went back to his Chair of Ancient History and started writing a book about Michel Psellos, a Byzantine monk, philosopher and chronicler of the eleventh century who was one of his favourite authors. He did not write to us, but as he liked drawing, he sent me a caricature showing a blood-thirsty Nestor bombarding a classroom of horrible hooligans with books of Herodotus and Tacitus. On the drawing, Nestor had written: "How to keep fit pending the next war!" The Toubib who had always made fun of Nestor said: *"That masterpiece will come out as early as 2453. Get your copy today."* I nonetheless believed that if there were to be any survivors, Nestor would be one of them.

What were we actually doing at the Zoo? We desperately tried to invent a better future but did not know if we really had the foresight or how far our folly might take us.

The most passionate dreamer of our group had been nicknamed 'The Bigamist.' He was a candid irreproachable guy, but his stunning girlfriend Claire had eyes of two different colours. He was bewildered by the fact that Claire had chosen him and panicked at the thought that somebody might steal her away from him. Gilbert said that her black eye turned his blood on fire, while I vouched having crossed Heaven's doors through her blue eye. We pretended to be bewitched by her, but the Bigamist became so upset by our little game that we decided to call it off. He had nothing to fear from us. We had a strict Code of Conduct that dictated that our friends' girlfriends could only be friends to us.

The Bigamist was happily in love and believed that happiness was something completely natural. Because he lived among courageous men and devoted women, he deeply trusted human virtues. He hoped that when the war was over, people of good faith would, hand in hand, re-build a world where justice and fraternity would prevail.

One night he started rambling about France: *"The soldiers of the previous war made two mistakes: they sold their weapons to merchants and, what is worse, they demobilized their brains. Stupidly they sat on the fence watching when in fact, they should have led the game."*

I was saddened by the blunt and miserable picture that my friends had of a country so dear to me. I wanted them to have a more balanced view. The Bigamist quoted a sentence from the "Lettre aux Anglais" of Bernanos which I had given him: *"Comprenons-nous ce que c'est que d'avoir manque une Paix?*[66]*"* and as he had some difficulties in pronouncing those French words I added: *"qui a coute cinq millions de morts?* He was mad at me for stealing the show. He yowled: *"The Lettre aux Anglais is addressed to me, not to you! In the future, I don't want you to read my letters!"*

I asked: *"How would an ignorant guy like you understand all those cabalistic signs on the paper if I had not spelled them out for you?"* But the Bigamist continued to dream aloud: *"We shall not fall into the same trap. At the first sign of peace, we shall over-mobilise, and this time things will be different...*

Gilbert's vision was less rosy: *"In times of peace, bastards always manage to be cleverer and slyer, and they are contagious. If we mix with them, we'll get infected and become bastards too!"* We were silent for a moment, but he went on: *"We should create little islands of resistance, where each group will fiercely defend those secret traditions whose very existence is under threat. There should be a difference between honest men and bloody bastards! The good ones need to know how to knock the bad ones down!"* Then, with that mocking arrogant mask which he would readily put on whenever caught being too serious, he asked: *"Maurice, will you be responsible for our African branch?*

"OK, provided you give me a day off tomorrow. I can't wait to set up my command post on top of the Kilimanjaro!"

Gilbert howled back: *"You, stupid idiot! That's the very first target the enemy will bomb! Air Marshal Rault, you know nothing about secret warfare. You are fired! You should apply for admission to the kindergarten school of the 'Maquis' for the grade of AC Plonk (temporary).*

"You're just an old ostrich! Your truths will be useless if you hide them away in a cave. Ok for the 'Maquis,' but it will only survive if it can send signals that

---

[66] *'Do we understand what it means to have missed a period of Peace which cost us five million dead?'*

are visible everywhere in the world. In Peacetime, Resistance must change; it should not be clandestine but flamboyant.

Gilbert was very fair play. He retorted *"OK, Air Marshal, we'll adopt your plans. Get your 'Maquis' organised, but nobody shoots until I light a torch on the Ben Nevis."*

Chapter Ten – Through Which Tortuous Pathways

During our debate, Gilbert had elevated me to the Capitol but only to throw me off the Tarpeian Rock![67] Luckily with a return ticket! The next day I found him, entirely at ease, rummaging through my books. To Gilbert, this was quite a natural. He firmly believed that his friends should benefit from everything he possessed and vice-versa. He suddenly stopped to read two lines of Homer which I had noted on the front page of a book: 'All this is the doing of the Gods. They have weaved a frame of Death for humans so there would be a song in the hearts of future races.'

He asked: *"Do you read Greek? Do you know Aeschylus?"*

"I studied his 'Agamemnon' and 'The Seven against Thebes' [68] *and found them so beautiful that I read his other tragedies."*

"How could you? In Greek, at most, I can cope with Xenophon[69] *in Loeb's edition, with its translation. But..."*

"But what?"

"Nothing!"

It was the first time that the impetuous Gilbert halted in the middle of a sentence. His mind seemed to drift away, and I did not insist.

We were entitled to a 48-hours' leave, which, thanks to the extraordinary way in which the RAF looked at things, in fact, lasted three days. In a slightly embarrassed manner, which was not quite like him, Gilbert tried to find out whether I really wanted to spend my free days in London. When I said no, he said: *"Then come to my place. The garden is beautiful, there are interesting walks, and you will tell me what you think of the library. Moreover, my dad will be delighted to meet a Hellenist"*. I had not thought about it before, but the word 'Hellenist' rang a bell: *"Is Sir Charles V...your father?"*

---

[67] *A rock on the side of the Capitol from which traitors were thrown off and killed.*
[68] *Two plays by Aeschylus, a famous Greek writer known as the father of Tragedy.*
[69] *Xenophon of Athens (430–354 BC) was an ancient Greek philosopher, historian, soldier and mercenary, and a student of Socrates.*

"Yes, don't tell me you know him!"

***

In 1940, one of my professors had lent me a small book by Charles V about Aeschylus. I had been thrilled by that book which seemed as innovative as 'The Origins of Tragedy' by Nietzsche but was closer to reality. I tried to find out whether the author had written other books but learned nothing more about him. His book remained unknown to most but was regularly ransacked by a few specialists, who did not always reveal their sources.

Gilbert told me that his father had been on the frontline during the whole of the 'Other War,' except during three stays in hospital, when his injuries had forced him to leave the front. I had also heard that he had always shown on the front that amazing bravery which his son had obviously inherited.

Gilbert added: *"I must warn you he is dying but still standing very straight in the face of Death."*

Although I had no doubt that Gilbert had invited me for his father's sake, I was deeply touched by the solicitude which this bird of prey was showing towards a dying man. At the Squadron, there was no room or time for feelings, and in normal circumstances, I would have refused. I was, however, curious to meet the man who had written such an admirable - albeit unrecognised - book and wanted to understand why its author had subsequently elected to withdraw into total silence.

***

On the train taking us to his home, Gilbert - as cheerful as a schoolboy on holidays – told me about those from whom he descended. *"Where we now live used to be a brigands' den. My ancestors made a living by plundering the Welsh or – but only in times of famine – their own compatriots, the Salopians!* [70] *Edmund V... decided to replace his lair with more comfortable lodgings. He called in Inigo Jones*[71]*, but just like the other V...'s, he believed that one did not need to learn to acquire knowledge. He intended to use Inigo Jones as a mere contractor, but when the latter protested, he dumped him.*

"Edmund then travelled to the Continent to look for a model befitting his dream house. It is said that he hardly looked at the palaces of Italy, Bohemia, and

---

[70] The people of Shropshire have been known as Salopians since the 17th century
[71] The famous British architect.

Austria and instead closely examined the beautiful ladies who lived there, sometimes even too closely. His method must have been as good as any other, as when he returned, he created V... Hall all by himself. Evelyn Waugh used to tell my father: 'What a superb setting for a beautiful woman.' Edmund's grandson, Philip called in another Jones, who had worked with Le Notre, to design the gardens. Jones II was more malleable than Inigo and Philip forced him to go against all the principles learnt from Le Notre. He made good the prejudice he suffered by increasing his fees. As Philip did not allow him to do anything, he would spend his whole days, sitting under an oak tree sipping Moselle wine. Now and again he would applaud Philip's fantasies, and Philip would say: 'That Jones, such a profound artist!' I do not know how good a landscaper he really was, but remember he was a bloody bastard.

"Oh, I forgot about Edmund. He was a visionary, and to house the three books he possessed - King James' Bible, a Book of Hours from the XV century and a venery guide - he built a huge library."

"We came too late to the book market to find original editions of Shakespeare, but as from the days of Pope and Swift, English literature is very well represented in our library. We even have a sizable collection of French and Italian authors. And don't forget, in the XX century, the V...'s finally discovered Antiquity. Shit!"

"What?"

"I wanted to surprise you, and I've told you everything. Too bad! Just imagine how your dream library would look like, and we'll see which one you like best."

I burst out laughing, and people in the compartment who had been listening attentively to Gilbert's ramblings followed suit. During the war, this was a very British way to applaud, and I hope they still do it. Gilbert went on: *"I have another surprise for Dad, and I must not miss that one. I did not tell him you knew them both."*

"Which both?"

"Dad and Aeschylus, bloody hell!"

Gilbert was triumphant as I fell into his trap: *"Listen, you say nothing until dessert. Then, at my signal, you cite Aeschylus."*

I felt he was gaining the upper hand over me and to save my dignity I ironically told a WREN who was caressing us with her smiles: *"And on top of that, I will have to buy him some lead soldiers."*

***

Three miles separated V...Hall from the station. At 160 paces per minute - an excellent appetizer - we walked towards the sun. It shone brightly in a desperate attempt to compensate for the decreasing warmth. Autumn was joyfully drying away the trees and made the forests look ablaze. They gave me a treat, almost as sumptuous as the one I enjoyed during a four-day train ride from the Atlantic's shores to Manitoba. I still miss the maple trees of Quebec, which back then, like princes dressed in crimson, had been my guard of honour.

As we entered the valley, V...Hall suddenly appeared looking like an Infanta, bathed in the purple glow of the sunset. Gilbert had mentioned a house and a garden. In fact, it was a Manor and a park, set in majestic surroundings near the Welsh border. It looked mysterious, secret, yet familiar! Had I already seen it in a novel by Walter Scott or Jane Austen? Everything that was so blatantly missing at Elsham was gathered there in this anthology: trees, fruits ripened by moon and sun, late birds, hand-trimmed lawns - so proud of being English - and those water features where early stars would soon start dancing…

The landscape, pampered since a thousand years, breathed out happiness and a butterfly, as though escaping from a Joan Miro painting, fluttered all around us. I said: *"This is the everything that Elsham isn't!"*

Somebody replied: *"Yes, but without Elsham, all this would be destroyed!"*

Leaning on his stick, Sir Charles V was waiting for us at the top of the steps. He looked just like Gilbert but devastated by time and thunder. He welcomed me most amicably but, almost immediately, withdrew into a place where he could not be followed.

At dinner, Gilbert finally got me to cite Aeschylus. Sir Charles awoke from his reverie: *"You know Aeschylus! Then how can you tolerate my illiterate son?*

"Sir, he probably knows many things he has never read about, but may I say, that thanks to you, I now have a better understanding of Greek tragedy."

Sir Charles nodded gravely and adopted me right away for the sake of Ancient Greece. He then vividly started telling me many anecdotes about his country estate.

Although Gilbert obviously knew all his stories, he stayed with us, as if drinking his father's words.

Sir Charles went on: *"I apologise if our Hall has no ghosts to offer you but it did house some visitors of flesh and blood almost as prestigious as the most famous revenants of Scotland. Do you know that Coleridge and Thackeray have slept in the room we have prepared for you?*

"One night, Coleridge, who was wandering in the park, talked for almost four hours about Hindu myths which he was making up while the drugs flowed around in his blood and fired his imagination. On the way back he found that his nightcap had been entirely destroyed by a puppy.

"A zealous housemaid barged in to say that there were two nightcaps in Mr. Hazlitt's room, but Mr. Hazlitt - who had been prevented by Coleridge from uttering a single word during the whole evening - was enjoying his revenge. He brutally replied: 'I always wear two nightcaps!'"

"Thus, at one o'clock in the morning, a groom was sent out on horseback to find a nightcap in the neighbouring mansions. When he returned, Coleridge was already snoring, but Hazlitt woke him up.

"Thackeray was hosted by my uncle Henry, but in return, the ruffian made a caricature of Henry in the 'Book of Snobs.' To punish him, Henry invited him anew and was even more attentive and caring. Thackeray who was furious and perplex modified his drawing to make it even darker.

"Henry had been waiting for that and sent him a card saying 'I have won. Knockout in the second round'. Thackeray probably conceded defeat as he sent no response.

"I'll skip the names of a few illustrious but forgotten men who also occupied your room. In my days Hilaire Belloc[72], Aldous Huxley[73] and Evelyn Waugh also slept there

"The first time Evelyn Waugh visited us, the lady sitting next to him at the dinner table said that Huxley had slept in his room before. He roared: 'I will not sleep with Aldous!' and sulked until we moved his luggage to another place. Waugh

---

[72] Joseph Hilaire Pierre René BELLOC was an Anglo-French writer and historian. Famous for his 'Cautionary tales for children.' He died in 1954.
[73] Aldous Huxley was an English writer, novelist and philosopher.

liked acting like a bear, but only to preserve his legend. Deep down he was a courteous and delicate man."

***

After dinner, Sir Charles asked to be excused, and Gilbert took me to the main lounge. It housed many beautiful pieces but, that night, all I saw was the portrait of a young woman hanging on the wall. She moved me so much that for one instant I thought she is too beautiful to be true, but then realized that it would have been impossible to make up that kind of face.

Gilbert said: *"She was my mother. She fell from a horse and died when I was four; it's strange to be older than one's own mother."*

There was nothing to add, but I just could not help wondering how many men had drowned in the depths of her eyes.

Gilbert guided me to the library. He looked like a magician having achieved an incredible trick. Edmund had designed the room as a prolonged oval, and the books were placed in undulating rows which made you want to follow them.

High glazed doors opened onto the garden as if to show that on the premises, research, action, and nature interacted continuously.

Of course, the value of a library does not consist of its structure but of the books which line its walls. Here, the most luxuriously bound books had no problems sitting next to Penguin editions purchased at £1 for forty books!

"Gilbert, is this is to prove that you are not as snobbish as people say you are?" I asked to tease him.

"Prove? Leave that to lawyers but tell me which one is the best, ours, or the one you dream about?"

"It's a draw!"

Treasures, accumulated there over three centuries, would have made the book lover that I am, happy for life. But upon seeing how greedily I moved from book to book, Gilbert said: *"Hey, I did not bring you here to play bookworms. Tomorrow we'll go walking."*

In those days, I used to fall asleep as soon as I closed my eyes but that night the face of Lady V lingered before me for a long time. A line from Webster haunted me: *'Cover her face; mine eyes dazzle; she died young.'*

The next morning, we left at dawn. It was one of those mornings where everything breathing under the sun exhales happiness. Every person we met along the way greeted us with friendly words. Drivers headed towards the same direction all proposed to give us a lift! Over and over again, vehicles would noisily brake next to us, with a lot of screeching and dangling metal noises but we wanted to walk. A girl, reminding me of fine Sevres china, overtook us in a big truck and reversed like a meteor to ask where we were going. A lady bus-conductor even stopped her bus and shouted: *"Hi! Free ride for our airmen!"* Six WAAFs packed in a jeep started screaming and whistling begging us to jump in and sit on their laps. After an intense but jolly discussion, they drove away howling like crazy Iroquois craving for a scalp.

Later on, a young girl driving a heavy horse-drawn carriage halted and asked us to travel part of our way with her. The girl and the horse looked so gentle that we were unable to refuse. We climbed next to her, and she insisted that I should take the reins. I'm glad she had enough good sense to pull them back when we nearly capsized into a ditch.

When we said goodbye, she gave us a basket of yellow apples and politely accepted, in return, the wilted red apples we had in our backpacks.

As I tried to explain Paddy's recipe to make fruits tastier, she invited us to raid her orchard whenever we wanted to.

Why is it that I can still clearly remember the huge hooves and large wise eyes of the dapple-grey horse, while the only things I can recall about the girl are her dimples and a strand of pale blonde hair dancing in the breeze?

***

When we walked back that night, we were tired but enjoying the feel-good factor that physical exercise can provide. Sir Charles had waited to dine with us. Gilbert showed him our itinerary on a map: *"We've walked thirty-six miles!"*

Sir Charles retorted: *"Not bad for amateurs!"* Then turning towards me he added: *"Sorry to repeat old stories you may already know, but I am desperately trying to fill the gaps in Gilbert's upbringing. Did you know about the Marathon Runners' predecessor?*

"When the Persian army landed in Greece, the Athenians sent a professional runner called Philippides to Sparta to ask for help. He covered the 150 miles of hazardous grounds which separate Athens from Sparta in less than two days. The Spartans did not hurry as according to their customs they had to wait for

the full moon! However, once they started moving, they did not linger. Soldiers in full armour holding their shield in one hand and a long spike in the other, walked fifty miles a day, for three days in a row. Before the 1914 War, I tried to do the same - wearing similar apparatus in similar conditions. The good peasants whom I met on the way thought I was a Martian and I had to reassure some policemen that I did not intend to conquer Wales.

"All this boosted my pride, and I kept on walking even though all the muscles in my body were begging for mercy. I managed to walk fifty miles on the first day but on the next, I abandoned my walk after forty-four miles. During the days which followed I had to climb the stairs backward, lifting my body with my arms and holding on to the ramp."

While he talked, Sir Charles seemed rejuvenated, and I almost forgot his age and impending death. He added: *"In Sparta, mothers armed their sons and when giving them their shields, would say 'return with it or on it!' To the Spartans abandoning one's shield was unforgivable infamy.'*

***

A bookshelf attracts me like a bright window in the night. Like a party where I knew I'd be welcomed even if I was not invited. The night before we left, I wanted to see the library one last time. Thinking that everybody was asleep, I walked in silently.

A lamp was lit at the far end. In its glow, I saw Sir Charles, slumped in his armchair. His emaciated neck - sagging between his broad shoulders - and ravaged face betrayed a man who had suffered too long and could not take it any longer.

I felt indiscreet and was about to withdraw on tiptoes when he called me firmly. As I sat next to him, he pulled himself up and asked: *"Are you looking for a book?"*

"I did not come to read but to look around!"

"Then please listen to me. Within six months I'll be dead, but that's not important! What is hard is that, before dying, I will have to bury my second son and my whole race. Gilbert is the last in the line!"

I was surprised: *"Why should he die? He has a good team and is an incomparable navigator."*

Sir Charles shook his head: *"What determines who survives? Talent or Luck?"*

"Luck for 90% but there are still 10% left for Talent. That's a lot, and Gilbert is a lucky guy."

"I think he has already used his last slice of luck. He has this crazy idea of completing sixty operations over Germany. Do you really think that a man can play Russian Roulette sixty times in a row without finding a bullet? In all big English undertakings, ever since William the Conqueror, in the conquest of the Empire and in all defensive wars, there has always been a V... on the firing lines. But this time is the last. This might mean that England will never really fight again."

"Not after your best war?"

"See what happened to France. It no longer exists. Too many dead in 1914 and not enough in 1940!"

I then thought about De Gaulle and protested: *"Come on, there is at least one Frenchman left, so nothing's lost yet."*

Sir Charles pursued his thoughts: *"I do not think we will know holocausts like in Verdun or Passchendaele.[74] But there is worse. This war is slaughtering an elite which took centuries to be built and will be so difficult to replace. If a bomb were to hit Elsham, killing ten 'Rampants', it would not be as dramatic as when a single pilot or navigator like Gilbert disappears! And they are the ones who get killed. What a mess. In twenty years, when England will need them most, they will no longer be there. To finance this war, we are spending everything we own abroad, but who cares? What's irreparable is that we are throwing the flower of British youth into the flames. Those flames which the world admires are in fact our own twilight!"*

"Sir Charles, I do not know if courage runs in the blood, but it can undoubtedly be boosted by a good example. Maybe you descend from the Black Prince but certainly not from Alexander the Great, King David or Scipio the African![75] However don't you think that your family's bravery has something to do with them?"

---

74 The Battle of Passchendaele, also known as the Third Battle of Ypres, was one of the bloodiest campaigns of the First World War.
75 Scipio the African was a Roman General and Statesman known for his love of conquest.

He smiled for the first time: *"I will ignore your insinuations about the virtue of my female ancestors; the more so as in the days of the Black Prince, the best families would have boasted about it. The graft of courage by example can only succeed if genetic courage still prevails."*

For a few seconds, he seemed to listen to a voice from afar but added: *"Many family dynasties had perished before us because they were exhausted.*

"I guess their demise was less painful because they had lost the will to live. But we are the opposite of a dying bloodline! James and Gilbert are some of the most valiant sons of this country, but I can no longer distinguish the living from the dead!"

James, Gilbert's elder brother, had been one of the famous 'Few.' A handful of young men who, by beating the Luftwaffe in 1940 had saved the World's freedom. In his Hurricane, he had shot down two Messerschmitt's and a Dornier before being killed in September 1940 while flying a Spitfire for the first time[76].

Sir Charles added sadly *"We are a tree which is being felled just as it bears its most gorgeous fruits!"* Sir Charles was shaken by a spasm of pain and ground his teeth to refrain from screaming. To be closer to his son, he had refused to take any painkillers.

I felt I should leave, but he insisted on showing me a letter, which Newman[77] had sent his grandfather. He tried to stand up, but the effort woke the monster eating away his insides. He fell back in his chair and grimaced saying: *"One day... perhaps one day..."*

In the silence, I could hear an ancient clock ticking at the other end of the library. Sir Charles added: *"God knows why I am telling you all this crap? Probably to keep away the only thing that really matters. I am three-quarters dead, and instead of taking care of my own soul, all I worry about is Gilbert's salvation!*

"Why is it more difficult for me to talk hear- to-heart to my son than it is to confide in the stranger you still were a few days ago? You know Gilbert. He

---

[76] *The original manuscript cites 14th September but the only Spitfire pilots killed that day were Sergeant Frantisek Marek and Sergeant Sidney Baxter.*

[77] *John Henry Newman (February 1801 to August 1890) was an Anglican priest, poet and theologian and later a Catholic cardinal, who was an important and controversial figure in the religious history of England.*

chases women and women chase him, and they get so enthusiastic about being caught! It's probably instinct but so much bed-hopping before meeting God..."

As I desperately wanted to comfort him, I said: *"Sir Charles, you are certainly aware that there is an Archangel who watches over our Squadron. While He sanctions six out of the seven capital sins, he does not seem to be bothered by Lust."*

"Why wouldn't' he?" Sir Charles looked at me, like a drowning man who sees his saviour on a bridge, about to throw him a buoy.

Words were becoming muddled in my brain. To try and think more clearly, I counted on my fingers. I added: *"Obviously we don't have enough time to become wise. What might look like Laziness is just the need for us to regain some energy before our next ordeal. Our appetite is too healthy to qualify as greediness and, despite the rumours, most of us stay sober. When we drink, it's not alcoholism it's just friendship.*

"Nobody is crazy enough to get drunk before an operation. Moreover, we are far too fragile to be arrogant, and there is nothing like Death to teach you humility.

"They say I am the most belligerent member of the Squadron, but none of our friends, members of our crews, Gilbert, or I know rancor, hatred or wrath! Not even towards the Germans! Neither are we envious. Last week a flight engineer saved a Lancaster from crashing. The medal was awarded to his pilot despite the latter's protests that he was not the one who deserved it. But guess what? The happiest man in the crew was the flight engineer! I am therefore convinced that our Archangel believes that lust has become minor in the circumstances."

Sir Charles stood up almost easily: *"Please Maurice, take good care of him, please protect him."*

"Sir, he's the one protecting me!"

GILBERT'S JOURNAL

MONDAY: Yesterday I might have said: *"Who's Hitler? I don't know him."* Tonight, however, our paths will cross again. On the first 'cookie'[78] which I

---

[78] *A 'Cookie' was a four-thousand-pound cylindrical bomb.*

dropped I had written 'To Adolph!' but he never acknowledged receipt. The blast probably blew away my message, but I still think he's a rogue!

I saw my dad and Maurice chatting a lot lately and shortly after - out of the blue - the Chaplain invites me to play squash with him. So blatant. The Chaplain plays perfect squash, but I'm sure he is part of a conspiracy to save my soul. If only they knew what kind of ally sits inside me.

The Chaplain has too much tact to preach to me, but that's his way of showing he is there if I need him. I wonder what he would say if in the midst of our next match I told him: *"Bless me, father, for I have sinned!"*

"How many times?"

"I can't recall."

"Me neither!"

Stupid joke. I'm sure he would tell me something extraordinary. His lips are always moving in prayer when we depart for an operation.

TUESDAY: I have given so much to the war and yet so little to you: Laura, Agnes, Claudia, Eileen, the two Mary's, the three Joan's, Monica, Annette and you, the anonymous girl from Ludlow. Your breasts were so hard that they made me forget your name. Come on idiot! Quit that circus NOW!

WEDNESDAY: Last night was hard, and I feel the snare is closing in. In Cologne, our right wing was pierced by a shell; in Stuttgart, a fighter scathed the left of our fuselage with his bullets; in Dortmund, the nose of our Lancaster was hit by flak and yesterday...

Oh, that burst of gunfire just under the astrodome! As if those four wounds to my aircraft are forming a circle around me. Inevitably, the sniper is now aiming, before he shoots.

THURSDAY: This may sound stupid or atrocious. I pray to God to take my father before me. Not to cut short his physical sufferings as I'm sure he's strong enough to endure them but because my own death would be too cruel to him. The most profound affection still glows in that old man, devastated by illness. When he braces himself to avoid moaning, those emotions become so intense they make him look desperate. Even then, he cannot express them.

THURSDAY: I am torn by conflicting emotions, squeezed between my body and my soul. I know old age often allows redemption, even after many lost battles, and I'm aging quickly. Not even two years have passed between the end of my teenage and the grave. It's as if every operation brings my death one year closer. War is claiming my body's worth, and now it wants to tear my soul apart. Apparently, the Pope used to give Plenary Indulgences to men killed in the Crusades. Probably the blood of the sinner could wash away his sins. Will God remember my battles?

FRIDAY: I hoped that Death would become something familiar. It doesn't. It's the other way around.

During my first operations, I would joke about it. Slowly I came to understand how tragic it could be. Yesterday, for a few moments, the pilot lost control of our aircraft. I almost panicked, and I just hate myself for having allowed fear to turn me into that poor dismayed creature.

I cannot forgive the things that frighten me. I thought my body had courage, so maybe it is my soul which has started to stagger. I feel I'm losing ground on those deadly nights. I don't have much to give, but whatever I have, I'll give You. I followed You in the Second Garden [79] and am now acquainted with fear, anguish and blood sweat.

SATURDAY: In four hours I'll go to the maps' room to be briefed for the next operation. Two hours from now, Death will once again start opening its snares. Annette, my sweetie, I badly want to run to you, marry you and, before leaving, give you the child and heir my father is longing for. More than me? No! Today I also have this burning desire to have a son of my own. I'm fed up with being the last of the Mohicans!

This brutal cry has betrayed me. I cherish the idea that you can, by giving me an heir, ensure that I do not entirely vanish from this world. Never mind, you know how to love, and I'm sure you will teach me. I won't be a hypocrite and tell you that I'm not coming because there are only so many things one can do in four hours. Time is not a problem, but I lack proper purpose. In flight, I won't even have time to think about you. But when I come back, I'll be closer to you and, hopefully, to God.

I have allowed many women to love me. If only for one silent hour, I had allowed myself to be loved by YOU. God, please let me survive once more.

---

[79] *Possible reference to the Garden of Gethsemane (the Second Garden) where it is said that Christ suffered to redeem the sins committed by Adam in the Garden of Eden (the First Garden)*

Will this operation exorcise my doubts and set me free to believe? I feel like shredded metal drawn by a magnet: "Christ the tiger, burning bright" and now I dare say: "Take my body Oh Lord, it's yours!" Desire, baptism, communion...maybe?"

Gilbert's journal ends on that unfinished sentence.

***

Gilbert went to the map room to check his calculations. Through the windows he watched an ominous orange glare filtering through the thick cumulus on the horizon. Iridescent under the spotlights, an oil spill, on the asphalt, reminded him of a decadent rainbow. The briefing was over. As Gilbert walked towards his Lancaster, dusk was already surrendering the sky to the first stars. The air disturbed as the first of the propellers began spinning rose like a hymn tuned to the tumult of the blood in his veins. Suddenly, he stopped. In a small puddle at his feet, he saw the reflection of Vega. She was distant and broken as if observed from the wrong end of a pair of binoculars. He felt this was a message which he tried to decipher, but his pilot was already calling. He hastened, vaguely worried at having perhaps missed a signal for which he had been waiting.

Bizarrely he told me: *"Once you've crossed the Red Sea you'll find the Promised Land."* Never before had he been so eager to live, and he started making his usual childish gestures to scare evil away. Although he vehemently denied it, they were his own personal spells to protect him from the greedy death lurking above. No one could tell from where the assaults would come. We had to do our best not to give in to the fighters hiding in their lairs. Before climbing into the aircraft, Gilbert memorized the position of every star. He wanted to be able to identify them even if the rest of the sky was hidden by clouds.

Four hours later, when he took his last readings, his chronometer indicated that it was midnight in Greenwich. He noted 0000 in the time column, on the extreme left of his logbook. He wanted to add 'Hello Sunday' but, by then, he only had ten seconds left to live. The last image on his retina, when the shell perforated the cockpit, was undoubtedly that of his aircraft, blooming into a huge rose of fire. A Kyrie perhaps or a Gloria which must have helped his soul to fly.

Chapter Eleven – Futile Requiem

The death of the Bigamist so soon after Gilbert's loss completely upset us, especially the Toubib. In his profession, he was used to seeing old or demented people die, but seeing men killed who were so young, so full of life and with so much to look forward to was both revolting and scandalous. To hide his grief from us and maybe from himself, he would rile against anything that came his way. On that day, according to Smithie, he apparently prescribed aspirin for diarrhoea and cough syrup for an ingrowing toenail. That was certainly untrue. Even during his worse outbursts against the absurdity of fate, the Toubib was thoroughly professional and extremely vigilant. However, as soon as he saw me, he howled from far:

"I am as stupid as you are!"

"Always boasting!"

"Listen, generally speaking, neither of us are superstitious. You, because you believe your God is fair and me, because I'm sure that two plus two equals four! Your God will not starve you if you are the thirteenth guest at a table or hurt you because a black cat crosses your way. To me, smashing a mirror or walking under a ladder will not mean I'll catch smallpox or cause one of my friends to die. Those causes certainly cannot provoke such results. Bullshit! We are as stupid as your gunner who wears his girlfriend's panties[80] to protect himself from bullets!"

"What Eddie does is not that stupid! In the Lanc's tail when he feels completely lost in the hostile icy night, the panties link him to a world of warmth and tenderness."

"Let me finish! In fact, I don't dare visit Claire alone. So, I thought that you and Nestor might come with me. Then I had second thoughts. You two should not go. You know why?"

---

[80] *Bomber Command crews would carry or wear any number of good luck charms, including one pilot who always flew wearing a pink apron and another who wore his favourite bobble hat.*

"Come on, spit it out!"

"I've been here since 1942. Before she met Francis, Claire was going out with another guy."

The poor Bigamist had suddenly been given back his real identity – Frank – as if flak had blown away his nickname along with his skin. The Toubib added: "That guy was also killed and I fear she might be contagious!"

"So, we're agreed on one point at least - you are a hand-sculpted fraud!"

"Don't try to play funny. I know how your people dance and wriggle their hips to bring rain to your island, and if you pretend that you don't have your own personal witchcraft, you're joking!"

"You're furious because your clients have chosen to travel thousands of miles away to meet Death and you will soon be redundant!"

"You want proof? Do you believe in Gremlins?"

Gremlins were cheeky hominids, about 15 inches tall, with long noses and huge protruding ears. They would secretly board our aircraft and play dirty tricks on our crews. We did not really believe in them but pretended to. To us, Gremlins were like homeopathy or vaccines.

They would break my pencil's lead, drop my compass in tricky corners, hide my ruler under my maps and at worse blur my radar screen - but never enough to make it unreadable. By nature, Gremlins could only cause repairable damages. Bomber Command had a vast directory of Gremlins' mischief, but no airman ever accused Gremlins of having killed a man. They were domesticated and controllable adversaries who we would use as shields to hide us from our real enemies – the ones who killed. At the end of the day Gremlins were on our side, just like elves and fairies but because the latter didn't trust aircraft, they sent their ugly cousins instead.

Of course, we always observed them while in flight, but I have never heard of a single case where a Gremlin was prevented from boarding one of our Lancs.

All that was small talk; just going on and on, to avoid tackling the real issue: should we visit Claire or respect her grief and her solitude? We looked towards the door as if the answer would come from there.

It was Nestor who walked in. He was mourning too. He did not frown but, unexpectedly, he talked: *"Going to see her will be difficult but failing to do so would be most unfair. We therefore decided to drop in to pay our respects, kiss her, and leave immediately after."*

It was Claire who begged us to stay. Her dormitory was similar to ours, with no chairs. We could have sat on the beds but chose to remain standing, fidgeting from one foot to another, like embarrassed schoolboys. Claire did not weep, but who could tell how deep into her soul her muffled cries were cutting? Amongst friends, it is often more comfortable to leave certain words unspoken, and in any case, none could have filled that heavy silence hanging over the void. I thought that because the Toubib was over thirty and Nestor had no age, they would find something to say. I then realised how unfair I was. In the face of Death, we were all like children, small and helpless.

Nestor proposed that we should go for a walk, saying he needed some fresh air. We followed the perimeter of the airfield for a while, but then headed towards the countryside.

Instinctively, we surrounded Claire like bodyguards, ready to protect her against any threat. Of course, we could protect her from ground attacks but would be totally useless against any blows dealt by fate.

Night had fallen. Mechanically I identified the stars of the first magnitude. They were all where they were meant to be, according to their invariable liturgy. Sitting on top of a tree, towards the West, Venus glowed green and splendid in the pink sky, but I resented her for having allowed Claire to suffer. I desperately rephrased sentences over and over in my brain, but they all sounded so pointless that I could have hit myself. Where could I have found a single word proving that the Bigamist was still alive in our hearts? I wanted to tell Claire that Francis deeply loved her, that since he had died as a hero, that love had become eternal but what a futile victory over Death that would be. My words might violate in Claire's own flesh her yearning for a lover now lost forever and, in whose arms, she had hoped to spend the rest of her life.

I then recalled what the Toubib had said about Claire's first boyfriend. Would she have the courage to fall in love a third time, or would any desire to love again necessarily die, in a heart so cruelly ravaged? I did not share my ramblings with Claire, as I could find no proper words to express them. Evading like a coward, I opted for shallow conversation. I told her about the legend of Orion, which glittered above our heads.

An Oracle had promised the blind Titan that he would see again if he managed to catch the Sun. Since millenaries, Orion incessantly paced the sky without ever losing faith. Could he be a symbol of hope in our distress? I then stopped, terrified that maybe, on another evening, I had already told her that same story. But she was not listening. She was also searching the sky, looking in vain for a star which had already burnt out.

Despite our clumsiness, Claire must have found some comfort in our company as, little by little, she seemed to relax. In fact, she was the one who voiced the only appropriate words spoken that evening. Women can show much more compassion than men, even when their grief is a thousand times deeper, and Claire found the strength to comfort us. As she kissed us goodnight, I naively said: *"Thank you for consoling us!"* She smiled faintly, but that smile was my reward.

A hundred yards away, the Toubib stopped and said: *"Strangely tonight I did not notice the colour of her eyes"* and I realised that I had also failed to do so. Usually, Nestor's gestures were very clear, but he made such a vague movement with his pipe that we could not tell whether he too had been unable to look into Claire's eyes.

***

Had Gilbert or the Bigamist survived, would our ideals have prevailed? Would we still be warming one another up in this cold world? I wonder, with them gone, I felt responsible for the Zoo, but very quickly my kaleidoscope was again shaken by Fate. I was projected far away from Elsham, to the Pathfinder Navigation Training Unit (PFNTU) at Warboys[81] and then onwards to Little Staughton to join 582 Squadron of Pathfinder Force[82].

---

[81] *Warboys was at the time commanded by the legendary Wing Commander Laurence Deane DSO DFC, who had been Maser Bomber for the ill-fated raid on Mailly-le-Camp. He signed Maurice's logbook at the end of his training as did another mercurial talent, Wing Commander Joe Northrop DSO DFC AFC, the Chief Flying Instructor (CFI).*

[82] *Only the very best crews were selected for Pathfinder Force and only the very best navigators. All were obliged to go through PFNTU. Pathfinders were chosen from the ranks of Main Force squadrons as a result of their performance on those squadrons, often after analysing bombing results, aiming point photographs and navigation plots. Since Pathfinders were responsible for finding and marking all Main Force targets, accurate navigation was key.*

A group photograph of 582 Sqn aircrew, taken in August 1945, probably to mark the cessation of hostilities.

By the time I started to integrate into my new squadron, the war was over. We became redundant and our Squadron had to be disbanded[83].

To my great despair, I was moved to Transport Command[84]. There, bureaucrats emerging from God knows where, very seriously tried to explain to the young wild wolves we still were, that the best we could do was to try and look elegant and parade like the members of the Civil Aviation fraternity.

***

I was impatient to be demobilised, as to me that meant real freedom. I was eager to be rid of my uniforms which after the war made me feel like a king without a kingdom. Unconsciously I think I wanted to be rid of everything to do with the war.

I am sad to say that after final demobilisation, unknowingly, unwillingly, silently but surely, life severed most of the bonds I had with my brothers in arms.

I am even sadder to know that with my mortal eyes I shall never see the torch on Ben Nevis.

---

[83] *Maurice and the Ross-Myring crew arrived at Little Staughton via PFNTU on 5th May 1945. The Squadron was disbanded on 10th September.*
[84] *Maurice was posted to 1332 HCU Transport Command.*

Chapter Twelve – Meanderings

I never dreamt of another life, but were those cravings to go to London, when I was on leave, part of another dream? During those hasty vacations, I escaped the far too stringent environment in which I lived, to taste the unbridled fantasy of London life. After five hours, my train would always reach King's Cross station by midnight.

I like London by day, but still feel more connected to the London I knew in the Black-Out, when she would, night after night, pull on her warrior's coat of darkness.

London reminded me of an immense train station to which lines from every corner of the World converged. King's Cross, which was my usual point of departure and arrival, was a squarely set example of the above, with, an added extra-planetary dimension.

Years after, in Tokyo, I stopped at the unimaginable station of Shinjuku. Its trains, crisscrossing on seven different levels, continuously gulped down and threw-up compact masses of human ants, always rushing to catch up with time. That station was a crazy cyclotron,[85] where every day, millions of souls were propelled and spun around without ever looking at one another. In this labyrinth, where the Japanese themselves sometimes lost their way, I asked myself whether the legendary Minotaur was nothing more but a greedy crowd, feeding off its own kind.

I must, however, say that from King's Cross at war, there oozed a special warmth – a friendly glance, or just a quick smile – between the men and women whose paths briefly crossed there.

In London, I would sometimes meet Smithie, one of the Navigators of the Zoo, who initiated me to a game which enchanted the 'Gavroche'[86] in him.

---

[85] *An apparatus where charged atomic and subatomic particles are accelerated by an alternating electric field while following an outward spiral or circular path in a magnetic field.*
[86] *Gavroche is a fictional character in the novel Les Misérables by Victor Hugo. He is a boy who lives on the streets of Paris and his name has become a synonym for a street child.*

In a bistro, he would approach a group of Londoners, pretending that London was a combat zone, which terrified us. He voiced his admiration for their amazing capacity to sustain so much pressure saying that what we wanted most was to return quickly to our Squadron where we would no longer be exposed to V1 and V2 rockets. His comments always boosted the locals who imperturbably continued to perform their routine tasks, in the fleeting shadows of those flying bombs. They would conclude - with a little modest look - that it was not as horrible as it sounded and that one just had to get used to it.

Most people were a far cry from realising that to rebalance the risks the German bombs were to the Squadron they would need to kill at least five million Londoners. In fact, the said missiles did not worry me much more than the thousands of crackers my Chinese friends in Mauritius fire to celebrate their New Year. In any case, we had been vaccinated against bombs.

Bombs were things we threw at others, and they would be breaking the rules if they were thrown at us. We might have been astonished to hear that bombs ignored that rule.

***

If I hardly noticed London's architecture in those days, it was perhaps because I was mesmerised by the hordes of different faces scurrying around me. I did not take any photos but faithfully entrusted them to my memory. They still return when I call them, dancing to and fro in the sunny days of my youth.

From the top floor of the London buses, I enjoyed watching its impressive fauna. It was as if the war had created hundreds of Mona Lisas for us to immortalise in the stronger cells of our brains. Swallowed by the crowd, they had the heart-rending charm of things you only see once. Like lovers saying good-bye on the brink of a totally uncertain future.

***

To me, living without poetry is like living without air. During hours on end, I enjoyed looking for French books in the bookstores of London and Cambridge. At the time they were rarer than the most elegant Champagne.

The first French book to force the 'Blockade' had been 'Le Crève Coeur' of Louis Aragon. Despite German prohibition, my friend Raymond Mortimer had

- almost miraculously - obtained a copy as early as 1942. He was so thrilled that he cheered: *"It's as if the Moon has sent me a present!"*

'Le Crève Coeur' was an artistic reply to Bir Hakeim, which had shaken within us, something deeper than sorrow. In a darkened Europe, people were leading the same combat as the one which had stopped Rommel in the Desert. Knowing that we had a poet in our ranks further reassured me and I learnt by heart the poem 'Liberté' of Paul Eluard. It lifted my spirits.

A Jewish friend who had been imprisoned in the sinister Francoist jail of 'Miranda del Ebro[87]' and had escaped through French Resistance networks, also sent me a few poems by Pierre Emmanuel.

He maintained that he had been cured of bacillary dysentery - contracted in jail - by simply reciting Emmanuel's 'Jour de Colère'!

I was fortunate to find, at Foyles, two books of Claudel: 'Tête d'Or' and 'La Ville.' I bought them at a discount because they were damaged. They had been rescued from a bombed-out house, whose occupants had unfortunately been killed.

Their heirs wanted to get rid of those scribblings, which meant nothing to them but were so precious to me. The thought that Claudel's books had survived the fire somehow inflamed me, but I could not help feeling sad about the previous owners of those books. I would sometimes see them, floating away in empty space, pale shadows reflected on a background of burned-out buildings with guts hanging out in protest.

Feverishly I waited for poets to find the right words to describe the urgency of those days. From South America, I could hear the loud voice of Bernanos, as if the volcanoes of Chimborazo and the Cotopaxi[88] had awoken to share their furor.

I dreamt that all the poets, painters and musicians of our World would compose a superb hymn with images of our times which, placed side by side like the letters of a mystical alphabet, might help our planet to stay alive.

I was thrilled to learn that one of the most generous poets to voice the pain and hopes of our times, was a fellow Mauritian, Loys Masson. We had become

---

[87] *From 1940-1947, Miranda de Ebro, a city in northern Spain, housed the central Spanish concentration camp/prison for foreign prisoners.*
[88] *The Chimborazo and Cotopaxi are currently inactive volcanoes in Equador.*

acquainted at the Royal College of Curepipe, and I really admired him. In a letter to our friend, Marcel Cabon, another Mauritian writer, he had written: *'Ici on fusille l'Etoile Polaire sur le front des héros!'* [89] It felt like a personal message, similar to those which the French 'Maquisards' used to send through the BBC and it urged me to fight with renewed vigour.

But no words moved me as much as the prophetical speeches of the General de Gaulle. From the vertiginous heights, where he had isolated himself, he unveiled a future which, to us, seemed trapped in an impenetrable fog.

The magazines 'Horizon' and 'La France Libre' nevertheless recognised in Louis Aragon - author of 'La Jeune Parque' - the first poet of the war and caused his precious little book to be re-edited in 750 copies.

On the 15th September 1942, for my 22nd birthday, I spent my last pennies on copy No. 536. When I first held that book, I felt the same euphoria which I subsequently knew when, in my sixties, as an ephemeral Head of State (whose main function was to preside over useless inaugurations), I resided temporarily at the Mauritian State House, the old 'Chateau du Réduit.'[90]

There - minimising all its other treasures – was a tiny piece of the Moon which the Americans had offered to the Government of Mauritius. It was just exhilarating to be able to hold it in my hands.

***

In the vast, free open-air theatre of King's Cross Station, anonymous and involuntary producers (just like ourselves) would stage many more Vaudevilles than tragedies, mostly to suit popular taste.

When my children ask me why I sometimes start giggling stupidly, without any apparent reason, it's just because a scene from those days suddenly pops up in front of me, for my eyes only.

Chance sometimes gave me a role in a scene where I briefly appeared without worrying about the rest of the intrigue or its outcome. One evening, I was waiting for the midnight train in the canteen of the station, when the demeanor of an air gunner, seated in front of me, caught my attention.

---

[89] *"Here, on the foreheads of heroes, it is the Polar Star which is being shot at."*
[90] *The residence of the former Governor General of Mauritius; now the official residence of the President of the Republic of Mauritius.*

Every two minutes he stood up, walked to the door, glanced furtively towards Platform Number One, and returned to his seat, looking more sinister by the minute. He finally asked me: *"Do you have a valid pass?"*

"Yes, and probably you don't?"

"No, I need to be back to base before noon, and those bloody leeches are stuck to the platform's barrier. I'll never get through!"

The leeches were, in fact, the Service Police – whose job, officially, was to enforce regulations, but whose real function and utmost pleasure were to embarrass the lower Military. Many would, with particular voracity, persecute those who absented themselves from their units without permission. They always went by two, like Siamese twins, bound by a membrane of indissoluble malice.

The air gunner added: *"Do me a favour: let's go out together. I'll try to sneak in while they check your papers."* His plan sounded childish. Tweedledum would verify my papers while Tweedledee would undoubtedly concentrate on the latecomer.

Fortunately, I recalled some of the tricks which my old friend Paddy used to play on the SPs. Because they were forced to fight their own humanity, most SPs had hardened and become allergic to friendship. Kindness almost suffocated them, and Paddy took advantage of this.

He would approach a pair of them on the pretext that he needed some information, and then, in his lofty Irish style, drag them unsuspectedly into a conversation, loaded with traps.

When, according to him, the policemen looked 'ripe enough', Paddy would throw in his joker: *"You know I really admire you,"* and, without giving them time to think twice, would add: *"I know a pub just around the corner which serves gorgeous whisky, and I would really be happy to give you a treat."* Imprisoned by their status, the police muttered that they were not allowed to drink on duty. That was not enough for Paddy. Rolling on, like an avalanche, he scraped his knife deeper into their wounds: *"I must warn you though: hold your left uppercut ready, or the waitresses will have you. They're the tastiest West End cannibals I know. Amazing plunging necklines and nipples popping out like bubbles of Champagne, just to tease you!"*

After getting the police to drool with envy, Paddy pulled on a sad face and naughtily pretended to show them how to reach that Eden of forbidden lust. What he gave them in fact was an address for the Salvation Army.

However, it was another trick of Paddy which inspired my strategy in the air gunner's case. After checking that all his papers were in impeccable order, Paddy would do something to catch the eyes of the SPs and pretend to desert. He ran away so clumsily that the policemen pursuing him would inevitably feast in advance on the prey they were about to catch. When they finally stopped him, Paddy wriggled and moaned and feigned so much panic that his face would certainly have softened a cheetah.

His captors' mouths watered as they rummaged through his papers. Stupefied to find that everything was in order, the only thing left for the SPs to do, was to walk away humbly but quickly, with their tails hanging between their legs. To embarrass them even further, Paddy - still the master of the grounds - would then publicly vent his indignation about how the police harassed so many innocent victims.

I thus proposed to adapt Paddy's strategy to the air gunner's needs. The SPs would just need to chase me far enough to allow my friend to cross the barrier. I walked towards them while he stood near the door, from where he could see without being seen.

Fifteen feet away from them, I suddenly turned back, as if startled, and ran away as fast as I could. They greedily took the bait. Howling like wolves, they rushed in to cut my path with their usual pincer tactic.

I would readily have hauled them down to the other side of London, but I did not want to miss my train. After forty yards, I finally allowed them to catch me. In a frightened voice, I asked: *"Is it me you are after?"*

"Who else? Your papers please!"

"No worries, they are fine."

"Then let us see them."

By then, the air gunner had been able to reach the platform and disappear into the crowd assaulting the train. I could have stopped the show there and then but was finding out how funny imitating Paddy turned out to be. I said *"Listen, guys, why so much fuss amongst people wearing the same uniform? Around the corner, there's a pub which serves the best rum from my Island; an incredible bouquet. Come, let me buy you a drink."*

The policemen almost choked at the thought of it. Desertion, attempting to escape, corruption of civil servants, the perfect charges. A dream come true.

After further simulated attempts at diversion, I proudly showed them my impeccable ID card and my pass. Flabbergasted, the SPs started fretting like sharks stranded on a sandbank:

"Then why did you run away?" I turned the tables again: *"I did not run away. Why should I?*

The SPs, though terribly embarrassed, tried clinging to the facts: *"Yes, you did run away."*

"Are you crazy? I simply ran back to look for my pen which I have dropped somewhere around here. A Black Swan, eighteen carats – why don't you help me to find it?"

With renewed motivation, the policemen desperately started looking for the non-existent pen. I added: *"Shit, somebody must have stolen it while you were losing my time. Why don't you start catching thieves instead?"*

I would have liked to tell the air gunner my story but suspected that if they saw us together, the SPs might smell a rat.

***

On an icy night in February, inside the station, I saw two men looking so incredibly alike that they had to be father and son. On his Navy uniform, the father wore a very rare decoration: the Conspicuous Gallantry Medal (CGM), reserved for those having accomplished a remarkable act of bravery. He looked as solid as a rock but his son - with his bright new pilot wings - seemed as vulnerable as fine crystal. Walking towards the platform, the youngest said: *"Dad, please take good care of yourself"* and I saw his father's eyes filling up with emotion and immense tenderness. Did he regret having transmitted to his son the urge to take the highest risks, without adding, for that purpose, the strength he needed to survive?

***

It is again at King's Cross that I was made to play, backstage, in a real drama, although my name was never mentioned.

On the last day of my leave, I treated myself by buying 'Regards sur le Monde Actuel' of Paul Valéry, which had just been re-edited. I was in the station's canteen, browsing through the book when I noticed a young woman staring at me from another table. When I looked back at her, she shyly looked away. The daring Amazon suddenly turned into a frightened Antilope.

Although her face tried to betray nothing, she looked intense and agitated. She stood up almost instantly and headed towards the platform. Five minutes later, I boarded the train.

I was desperately trying to find a seat when she walked towards me from another car and said: *"Please follow me, there's still some free space where I'm sitting."* She spoke perfect French without the slightest accent.

On her officer's uniform, I saw a badge I had never seen before: F.A.N.Y.[91] The ability to book a seat, on such a packed train, was without any doubt the doing of the Amazon, not of the Antilope. I docilely followed her.

As we sat down, she said: *"You know I don't usually talk to strangers, but then I do not often meet navigators reading Paul Valéry!"*

"Blessed be the good Paul who gave me the chance to meet you!"

"I do not know the book you have."

"Good, let's discover it together."

The locomotive hooted. It was midnight, the time at which trains, worldwide, change their hooting and perhaps even change tracks. Towards what adventures was this train leading us? Lighting in the car was weak and bluish, making the other passengers look remote, almost ghostly.

The Amazon decided that we should open the book haphazardly - eyes closed - to see who would find the most amazing quote. She started: *"Unbeatable, I have an Ace, see!"* With her finger, she underlined a phrase where History was being thrown to the dogs because it engendered false memories, leading nations to feel outrageously powerful or persecuted. Then came my turn: *"My Joker beats your Ace!* She read: 'At the outset Politics was the art of stopping people from meddling with matters which concerned them. To that was later added the art of forcing people to decide matters they do not understand'."

---

[91] *F.A.N.Y stands for First Aid Nursing Yeomanry formed in 1907. Some Special Operations Executive (SOE) agents were recruited from the ranks of the F.A.N.Y though this did not become public until long after the war.*

"Oh, you're cheating! You turned the page over to add the second sentence".

"No, totally legitimate. The second sentence cannot be severed from the first."

"OK. Let's say, Deuce. Whoever wins the next turn, wins everything!"

She showed no trace of fear and looked like a carefree schoolgirl. There seemed to be so much energy and enthusiasm running in her veins that she could not possibly believe in death.

The beam from the pale little lamp above was cozily wrapping us in a luminous cone. That made us feel even more intimate as - in order not to bother the other occupants, we were both whispering as if performing a secret ritual. The only ones awake in our car being Valéry, the Amazon and me.

Suddenly she opened a page where the words 'the war' printed in bold caught our eyes. The charm broke instantly, and in the silence, an ominous shadow crept in between us. Deep inside her eyes, I could see ravaging nausea which invaded some of us before a difficult mission. Because I had associated her with poets – not war – I had grossly failed to measure the degree of anguish lurking inside her.

After seeing her joy die so brutally, how could I have been so blind in failing to decipher those very familiar signs? I could see how disturbed she looked but was unable to figure out the right reasons. I did not understand that she was directly involved in the war and stupidly concluded that she was merely trembling for somebody she loved.

The train stopped in Peterborough. As she bade me farewell, she made a valiant effort to recover her previous tone of playful comradeship, and I failed to understand that her true feelings were being undoubtedly stifled by the imminence of some atrocious tribulation. Many months later, I learnt that F.A.N.Y., the intriguing acronym I had seen on her uniform, were often secret agents parachuted into enemy territory to help the 'Maquis'! (a subtle English paradox to mark their spies with distinctive badges, a ruse which the Germans never unmasked).

My Amazon was certainly using her perfect knowledge of the French language to serve her country bravely, and this was no doubt why she had been chosen for that kind of operation. I guessed that when we met, she was preparing herself to jump into the void with a will which would not be stopped but could not prevent her body from quivering with fear and apprehension. On the brink of vertigo, she had endeavoured to find in glimpses of peaceful days, and in the bliss of being acquainted with great poets, a remedy against the cruel reality of her current life.

I do not know what became of her. Did the Amazon succeed in her perilous adventures or did the Antilope - too frail to escape her evil predators - know a painful and lonely death in the Gestapo's jails?

***

In the encounters described above, Chance always guided me. Duty, which had led me to live abroad, sometimes lent me some strange powers. Although I had decided to play my life on arbitrary operations, like that of an author writing his first book, I have always chosen my own routes, as and when they opened up before me.

At first, I had been a bit taken aback by the Londoners' incapacity to understand where I came from and cannot recall how many times they asked me whether I was Spanish, Greek, Lebanese, Indian, Maltese, Brazilian or Jewish.

More than a hundred times I tried to explain from where I came: *"Mauritius is the third island between the Cape of Good Hope and Australia,"* but I finally gave up.

To avoid answering the same annoying questions whenever I went to London, I pretended on each trip to be a different person with a new personality and resolved to wake up every day as a citizen of a different country.

I soon realised what benefits I could draw from my cosmopolitan looks. Under a pseudo, with new imaginary origins and a revised biography, I opened myself up to experiences totally defying my original character. Looking for adventures in displacement alone would have been naïve. Just travelling from place to place was an ambush for simple minded people. Why change countries if you cannot change your mindset? I did not want to disdain all the opportunities that London at war could offer.

What better crossroads than Piccadilly Circus or Marble Arch to allow myself, feeling like a bohemian, to slide into time gaps, not really knowing what I would find on the other side. After all, by so doing, I was only imitating Ulysses, my childhood friend.

One of our traditions at the Zoo was to play some crazy tricks, just before going on an operation, to confuse the spies of Death. I enjoyed those impersonations and wanted to make the most of those pleasures which could disappear at any time.

I thus made people believe that I was a Red Indian, an Eskimo or a cousin of Haile Selassie. It was very easy to pretend that I came from Persia as one of my ancestors was Persian. Most of my interlocutors were so naïvely ignorant of Geography and History that it was not difficult to make them believe that I belonged to mythical or even extinct races.

I however lamentably failed in convincing a railway-man, at Elephant and Castle station, that I was a giant Pygmy. Similarly, near Pimlico, an attorney's clerk (a fundamentally suspicious species) vehemently denied that I came from Atlantis.

On the other hand, it was reported to me that a municipal clerk, from Camden Town, maintained that an Aztec of Royal blood, engaged in the RAF, had told him some surprising secrets about Montezuma. There was also that stenographer from Finsbury Park who kept boasting - with supporting evidence - that she had known a real Trojan. Most of all I will never forget that hilarious night where I pretended to be a Tibetan in Tottenham.

***

As soon as I would board the train back to base, the curtain would come down, and the fiction immediately vanish. It was probably a form of secret revenge over all those comfortably seated people, whose chances to grow old, were so much better than mine.

***

I doubt that the World will ever be able to regroup, in the same place, the vast variety of human types which one could find around London at war and nothing in its ruins allowed me to guess how prestigious its future would be.

Among the soldiers boarding the trains, many would in fact, via the runways of an island transformed into a giant aircraft carrier, be heading to their graves.

No one could guess who those would be. Except maybe for a slight stagger in the gait, unconsciously affected by the weight of imminent death, no sign would betray those strong and healthy 'walking dead.'

They would fly from the airfields of those nights, never to return. They mingled amongst us with the discretion of illegal immigrants. Maybe they had already mastered the art of going around unnoticed.

***

It was to London that all the countries who wanted a free and fair world would send their soldiers, as Ambassadors. Soldiers under so many different uniforms swarmed the city's streets. Most were British or American, but there was also many Canadians, French, Belgians, Dutch, Norwegians, Australians and Czechs. Slightly cut off from the others were the Poles. For some reason - unknown to me - many did not trust them and treated them with disdain. They wore strange berets which made them look a little alien and their aloof or bitter faces somehow betrayed how exiled they felt in those days. They had been the first ones to face the enemy, and now, a universal ploy of silence and cowardice was ousting them from the winners' camp!

Did politicians believe that they would be able to reconstruct the World on a nation's despair? Something warned me that Peace might be lost if all that Poland deserved for showing so much resistance and heroism was ripped away from it. During the very courageous and noble Warsaw Uprising[92], I really felt revolted by the atrocious plot set up by the Russians, who deliberately halted their tanks to give the SS enough time to slaughter their Polish allies.[93]

I went to see my boss and told him: *"The RAF will surely fly to Warsaw's rescue. Please enroll me as a volunteer."* He looked at me thoughtfully and asked: *"Do you know where Warsaw is?"*

"I know one thing which you seem to have forgotten: Warsaw is in Europe!"

My impertinence made him smile, and he said: *"I have not indeed dwelt on this but going there means crossing the whole of Germany and about half of Poland! At least a six-hour flight. Let's assume we can do it. Of course, there are some Russian airfields only fifteen minutes away. If we could land there, that mission would have been tricky but not impossible.*

But, unfortunately in Warsaw, just as in Katyn[94], the Russians want the Poles to be exterminated and are refusing to give us permission to land. The flight will

---

[92] *The Warsaw Uprising in 1944 was a major underground attack by the Polish Resistance Home Army to free Warsaw from Nazi occupation. During that heroic but tragic uprising which lasted 63 days, the Germans killed about 160,000 people including thousands of children.*

[93] *In April 1939, Russia, Britain and France met to form an alliance to defend Poland - but by August 1939, Russia made a pact with Germany. Through the Nazi-Soviet Pact, Stalin and Hitler agreed not to go to war with each other and to split Poland between them. It is believed that at the end of WW2, the progress of the Russian troops was deliberately delayed to enable the Germans to kill more Poles.*

[94] *The Katyn massacre was the name given to a series of mass executions of Polish nationals carried out by the NKVD in April and May 1940.*

thus last at least twelve hours instead of the usual six. Having to carry double loads of fuel will leave no space for useful cargo. A few boxes of medicine and some machine guns at most. By then, our aircraft will be like sitting ducks with almost no chance to return safely home. Moreover, the risk that it will be the Germans who will grab whatever we are able to drop is very high. We cannot afford such a luxury!"

"Loyalty is not luxury! I know that the German-Soviet pact regarding Poland still survives. But if Hitler and Stalin both agree to slaughter Poland, why should we keep our arms crossed and become their passive accomplices?"

"Believe me, I would like to go there too, but it's out of the question. The best we can do for those poor guys is to keep on bombarding the Germans wherever we can hit them."

***

Returning to London years later, I discovered so many monuments which I must have passed by a hundred times, without really looking at them. Was it because in those days, London was the capital city of Freedom that I chose to keep my eyes shut?

Chapter Thirteen – Equinox

Hiroshima caused those duties - which had made us so proud - to become irrelevant. But I refuse to grant the Bomb any retroactive value. Every time we killed we risked our own skins. The Squadrons to which I belonged were depleted by over 50%. To allow one of us to survive, at least another had to die. We, therefore, have no reason whatsoever to feel ashamed or guilty.

***

When ex-Bomber Command comrades meet, we always enjoy chatting about our operations in the RAF. However, I don't know why I never told anyone what happened on the 21st March 1945 close to Bremen at dawn at 20,000 feet. Whenever memories of that operation came back to haunt me, I mercilessly buried them deep inside as if the proper time to face them had not yet arrived.

Furthermore, something told me that the game was not completely over. Those vibrant souvenirs continued to live within my soul - like seeds under the soil – secretly hoping that in a future spring they might be able to bloom. The game was still being played and the choice was mine.

Once, however, shortly after the war, I thought that I was finally ready. I was attending a talk, about Jouve,[95] at the French Institute of London. On stage, Stephen Spender was stretching out his long invertebrate limbs like a large red octopus. He sharply contrasted with the solid little man who was pursuing a haughty monologue, before an audience of respectful but astonished English ladies.

Four verses of the poet suddenly hit me: They ran:

'Because we chose to be the stronger angels

Coming from the deep island of storms

Flying everywhere, dropping on the thrash

The weight of mystical steel and destruction'

I was beginning to understand what he tried to say when something bounced hard inside my heart. I did not hear a single word from the rest of the talk and

---

[95] *Pierre Jean JOUVE was one of France's first poetic voices. His career spanned decades. He died in 1976.*

do not know how I returned to my lodgings. During the days that followed, I kept wandering around London like a boxer after a knock-out.

In those days, having discarded the khaki or greyish camouflage dress they wore to play at war, demobilised young women were finally showing the sun how beautiful they really were. They bloomed in every street like shiny colourful flowers. But strangely I did not even look at them.

While I walked amidst those vivid symbols of Peace, my mind strayed to the abstract and geometrical spaces of the Lincolnshire, where long irrigation canals interconnected triangular airfields. Somehow, those verses were giving me a chance to understand that my ghosts, in fact, originated from their runways.

***

As time went by, those thoughts slowly faded away, but sometimes, for a few seconds, I would have a fleeting vision, impossible to capture. It, however, gave me hope that I would, one day, be able to bring into broad daylight the mysterious figure which kept haunting me and see his face at last.

Twenty-one years later, same date, same time, in an ambiguous zone between dreams and consciousness, a man was there. He had waited a long time - but time did not matter to him - and he was now telling me that we had an account to settle. Although my visitor had no face and I had never seen him before, I recognised him straight away.

From the most intimate parts of my memory a voice – which I had never really heard - was now asking the question I had been evading for so long: *"You remember our deal, that equitable sharing: Life for you, Death for me?"*

Since the visitor had decided to come, at last, I accepted to face him. Let's review, step by step, what happened at the time.

In early 1945, Bomber Command was fine-tuning a new strategy around 'Dawn Assaults' in the cruel game we had to play with German towns. Throughout the night, small groups of aircraft simulated attacks on enemy lines. They carried nothing but loads of silvery paper strips, which they dropped in the air. The echoes which they triggered on enemy radar screens were similar to that of an important raid of bombers. The German defences, therefore, readied themselves for attack and fighters were scrambled to intercept. But once in the air, all they could catch were thousands of pieces of shiny confetti![96]

After having spent a harassing night chasing ghosts, the enemy defences would then cede to the perfidious promises of dawn, which sometimes make dying men believe that they might survive.

It was at that precise moment that the real attacks would be launched, bursting out from the sea and the darkness, like a nightmare! The heavy black bombers simply needed to finish off a prey which had by then become far too nervous and exhausted to defend itself. The big inconvenience of that method was the return journey which necessarily took place in broad daylight.

The Lancaster which would sacrifice everything to its bombing power - carried three times as many bombs as the American aircraft but definitely lacked adequate defensive armament. It only had eight light machine-guns compared to the thirteen heavy cannons of the Fortresses[97]. A Lancaster seen was a Lancaster down! Those bombers had been designed to operate at night. On their way back, deprived of the protection of darkness, our squadrons always ran the risk of being massacred by enemy fighters

That is when a smart fat ass at Headquarters suddenly remembered the Mustang. Because it was less manageable than the Spitfire, not as swift as the Thunderbolt and not as heavily armed as the Typhoon, the Mustang was for long seen as the Cinderella of fighter groups. Nonetheless, it possessed a clever mixture of all its glorious rivals' attributes and had an extraordinary flying range. The Mustang could thus wander very far into the heart of Germany to rescue injured bombers as they limped back to base. Thanks to the Mustang, dawn raids became profitable.

**

On the 21st March 1945, our mission was to demolish all the railway infrastructures of Bremen at sunrise. As we neared the enemy lines, I checked

---

[96] *The 'shiny confetti' to which Maurice refers was called 'Window' – strips of metal dropped from the sky that played havoc with German radar. They were often carried by small groups of aircraft, as well as being dropped by the 'Main Force' bombers at certain points of a raid. This was one of many 'spoof' tactics deployed during the war to confound the German defences.*

[97] *Standard defensive armament for an Avro Lancaster was eight Browning .303in calibre machine guns – four in the rear turret, two in the dorsal turret, and two in the front turret. The B17 Flying Fortress had much heavier calibre 0.5in machine guns (the 'G' model had now less than 13) with greater range and hitting power.*

on my map the red circles indicating concentrations of flak. I had never seen so many around a target. Obviously, Bremen had no intention of surrendering.

As a rule, I never looked outside when we were being shot at. This would have served no useful purpose and could further affect the accuracy of my calculations.

When things got really hot, I always remained behind the black curtain isolating the navigation cabin. I forced myself to see in the war no more than an obligation to find the speed and direction of the winds.

On that day, however, messages received from our air gunners to signal the location of flak batteries sounded increasingly anguished. Giving in to curiosity - which I had successfully resisted so far - I went to the nose of the Lancaster to see what was going on. I was petrified. We were in Dante's Inferno! Like a dragon refusing to die alone, Bremen was spitting out its hatred through thousands of blazing cannons. A massive wall of thick flak was protecting the target. From where we were, it seemed impossible for even a tiny sparrow to fly through that wall of flames.

The deadly brownish flares of the explosions clogged to one another. In the early dawn, we had no choice but to dive – as if naked - into that chasm of fire. As we came closer, we could see that the wall was not entirely impenetrable. Despite the density of the flak barrage, there were still a few gaps through which some lucky ones might be able to sneak through. Some would stay behind to allow others to pass. On that day, I wondered how many amongst us, would be chosen to pay the fire's ransom?

About 200 yards ahead, headed on the same course, but slightly higher than us, another Lancaster was approaching the wall. As it got closer to the line of fire, it brusquely dived towards the starboard, where the explosions seemed less intense.

At that precise moment, a whole part of the wall collapsed, rolling away like a wave but immediately closed back, right on the track of the wretched plane.

At that very moment a gap opened right in front of us and our pilot, Johnnie, threw our aircraft into that 'peaceful' channel between the blazing clouds. The other Lancaster desperately zigzagged, in an attempt to escape the surrounding bursts of shrapnel, but suddenly, hit with full force, it exploded and disintegrated in the air. Shockingly, as I watched those debris of mixed metal and flesh falling to the ground, I felt no fear, no pity, and no guilt.

What I then felt then, was so unexpected and so weird, that I could not name it. As if I had fallen out of the game, lost my humanity and had, once and for all, paid my tribute to flak.

We dropped all our bombs and the town was ablaze. Satisfied, I went back to my radar screens. After several complicated manoeuvres to trace and avoid enemy fighters, we finally headed towards the coast.

We had just reached the shoreline when our rear-gunner Eddie shouted into the microphone: *"Fighters behind us!"* - Somebody asked: *"Whose fighters?"* The question sounded so naïve: if they were behind us, they could only be German. After a while, Eddie replied: *"They are Long-nosed Focke-Wulf, the most venomous type!"*[98]

Who would they choose this time? Who, amongst us, would play the lightning rods? Eddie put an end to my speculations: *"There's one heading straight at us!"*

It is indeed a paradox that the best defense of a bomber, tracked by a fighter, should be its slowness. That slowness caused the relative speed of the fighter to increase. This accordingly shortened the time during which the assailant could actually aim and fire before having to take evasive action. I called Johnnie a last time to remind him that for us, acceleration meant suicide.

I had lengthily explained to the air gunners that firing from a distance of over 800 yards would only show the opponent that we were panicking. Eddie shouted *"1,500 yards!"* Watching the Focke-Wulf in his sights, he had started the countdown.

Hastily I scribbled my last observations in the logbook: 0608 GMT. Altitude 20,000, Course 265o. Latitude 53.22N. Longitude 05.18E. Wind 306/52. A strange testament indeed!

"1,200 yards!" We were flying at a relative speed of about 120 yards per second. Some 18,000ft below, the North Sea gaped at us; 18,000ft of spinning before hitting the water. Eddie proclaimed that during our previous raid, a bomber, which had crashed like a torch into those icy waves, had continued to burn below the surface.

---

[98] *The Focke Wulf Fw190D was the most successful of its type and could compete with the latest mark of Spitfire and Mustang on equal terms.*

I would have liked to see the film of my life before drowning. But from my past, the only thing I could recall was the bright cheeky eyes of a girl who touched me, one evening in a distant country. Was this what my life was all about? A tiny piece of sky filtered by soft eyelashes?

"1,000 yards!"

Within eight seconds the die would be cast. To offer the least possible surface to the bullets, I rolled myself up, pulling my knees under my chin. The posture of the foetus in its mother's womb. Would I ever be reborn?

I still watched the air speed indicator to be able to warn to Johnnie, in case he yielded to his instinct to throttle up. If the air gunners panicked and started shooting too soon, any intervention would come too late as it would then be impossible to unlock their fingers from the triggers.

"800 yards!"

Vertigo! The world is upside down! Pulling on all his muscles, Johnnie, our rugby champion, threw our bomber into such a narrow spin that I felt my guts pushing up my throat. Instead of diving, as prescribed by the manuals, he had spiraled upwards, on the edge of stalling. Taken aback, the Focke-Wulf was unable to latch on to us. Fortunately, we were spared the furious screeching noises caused by the whiplash of bullets on our fuselage which can cause eardrums to explode.

The Focke-Wulf had to let go but immediately launched another attack. It would not be fooled so easily a second time, but we needed to play the game to the very end.

Belatedly remorseful, I realised that while being wholly concentrated on surviving, I had confused the Pater and the Ave, and stammered: *"Forgive us, poor sinners"*. Then turning to my guardian angel, who hopefully had enough humor to accept some irreverence, I yelled: *"Hey, please do something for me. Can't you see I'm busy?"* For the second time, I felt the presence of the Dead Navigator. Before even hearing the first word shouted by Johnnie, I knew he would announce salvation.

"Mustangs to starboard!"

More shaken by joy than danger, how could I stop the urge to look at our saviours? As I pulled back my black curtain, I saw the Mustangs. The extra fuel tanks which they were dropping to facilitate their combat, reflected the sun while falling, looking like swords of fire under their wings.

If ever I am able to recompose a day made up of my finest hours, I would place, close to the middle, the moment when the Mustangs did their luminous gesture, while the broad wings of our Lancaster slid towards them like a greedy sunflower.

Johnnie shouted: *"Navigator, I'm turning towards them."*

"Yes, dive to 2,000 feet, and take a 10 degree course to port to compensate drifting."

I thought to myself: *"You little jester!"*

In fact, the dive was a good move. Either the Focke-Wulf allowed us to slip away, or when coming down behind us, decided to concede to the Mustangs the benefit of altitude in the deadly carousel which was about to start.

On the other hand, given our combined speeds and the short distance between us, turning to port would not have spared us a single bullet. It was with those little devices that I unofficially gained the respect of my crew members. It makes me happy to think that I somehow shared in guiding them. The Focke-Wulf's pilot was a conscientious guy. He dived behind us again and executed another pass in over speed, but already knew he had lost it. He needed to keep an eye on the Mustangs flying at full throttle. Firing his tracers far beyond our aircraft, was only a gesture of frustration.

Not to be beaten, the irrepressible Eddie, triggering all his toys, was howling swearwords that would have caused a sergeant-major to blush. Behind us, the Mustang's had taken over. The curve of the globe was already masking the tall flames that Bremen was hurling towards the sky. I stiffened, then stretched my limbs, to resist the sweet lotus taste of the coming dawn. We were still in an area where fighters lurked, but every minute took us closer to places where death no longer preyed. Outside, powerful sound walls created by our four undefeated engines resounded like the ovations of a cheering crowd. Our propellers, fiercer than thoroughbreds, were flying us back to base.

I forced myself to stay awake by manipulating my instruments, but all my senses craved to fall into a deep sleep, like Ulysses on Nausicaa's[99] beach. Difficult to resist that welcoming dawn. Lightheaded, as if floating on thin air, I dreamt that I was linked to the earth by ties as soft as silk under my lips.

---

[99] *Nausicaa is a princess who rescues Ulysses on a beach after a shipwreck.*

Navigation itself seemed almost too easy. I could receive clear signals transmitted through the secret channel of Reims. They danced on my screen like phosphorescent nymphs. Those sweet green dancers, who had guided me through deadly forests, were now waving from the high grass, inviting me to follow them to their luminescent country. Being alive can bring violent pleasures, like those of a wild beast scenting its prey.

It must have been in those days that I swore to be faithful to the earth and dedicated to you - whom I did not know yet – a hymn of grace which meant: 'The world is so beautiful my love, so beautiful!'

I did not know that every turn of the propellers would bring me closer to another dawn, lost in a remote future, where the men who had fallen back there, would come back to ask: *"What did you do to us?"*

Chapter Fourteen – Clearer Skies

Until the very last combats, the resistance of the Luftwaffe never let go of its hatred. In the final weeks, we even had a red alert. Messerschmitt Me262 fighters were being reported in many places. This type of jet fighter, which the enemy managed to produce well ahead of us, was highly superior to any fighter we had to oppose it. Even if it could not succeed in snatching our victory away, it might still inflict very cruel losses to our squadrons.

Once they had taken off, they seemed invincible. We only had one objective: stop them from flying. RAF Fighters and bombers combined their forces to blow up the jets' shelters with bombs and rockets, turn their runways into lunar craters and burn away their stocks of gasoline. Pinned to the ground, those terrible birds of prey would be unable to exert their tremendously devastating power.

As the Reich of a Thousand Years dramatically shrunk, both the Wehrmacht and Luftwaffe agreed to give absolute priority to the withdrawal of their anti-aircraft weapons. Those weapons were being concentrated in areas which got smaller by the day. In our nightmares, we watched Germany gradually turning into a single monstrous anti-aircraft battery. It fiercely tried to send back to the sky the destruction falling from it. It was only in the second fortnight of April that, at long last, the enemy started to look beaten.

Bomber Command had been a big oak tree, depleted by every raid, but by then it was almost in control of the storm.

For our last operation, the objective was Berchtesgaden. Rumor had it that some important Nazis, and perhaps Hitler himself, were nesting there. We had heard that Hitler had committed suicide, but some people at Headquarters could not believe that the Werewolf had indeed died. Excited by the prospect of bombarding the heart of the Nazi myth, we could not wait to blow up everything. In flight, a wireless message, however, informed us that General Leclerc's guys had progressed so quickly, that our bombs might land at the wrong address and hurt them.

During that raid, only one battery fired at us. That inappropriate gesture provoked strong argument on our way back.

"Must be the Americans; they alone can be such frauds."

"What Americans? It was the Russians!"

I hoped there would be some children left, as we had some exciting tales to tell them. We had probably avoided one of the opening shots of the World War Three!

***

And what about the Germans? Casually, elegantly, we had already put them to one side.

***

Bomber Command saw technical unemployment coming up. We kept repeating the last insult dedicated to the Butcher - with love - *"Hush! He is eating up his maps as he can no longer find any cities to flatten."* Some predicted that his next coup would be sending 2,000 bombers to Moscow!

Each operation always brought its spark of happiness, and we kept hoping that Victory - by gloriously removing all dangers - would be a burst of unequaled joy. On 8 May 1945 it was not Germany alone, but Death itself, which, trapped in its own snares, capitulated unconditionally.

Sadly, Victory over the forces of evil did not last long. The troops' fighting spirit vanished as they were demobilised. Roosevelt was battling to help the Russian Czar, while Churchill wriggled in the shallows of Peace like a stranded whale. Utterly disgusted by the exigencies of the 'Societé de Consommation,' De Gaulle himself looked beaten, dropping his long-dislocated arms in despair as he spoke.

We were not vigilant enough. Death managed to escape and is hounding us once again. Deprived of our chiefs, I fear we may lose another war of fire.

***

As soon as Peace prevailed, we were assigned to the joyous 'Operation Exodus.' We would fly to the Continent to repatriate freshly liberated prisoners of war, and I had the opportunity to land, in France, for the first time.

Since the sky was all ours, taking off was even more pleasant than landing. I no longer needed to close my black curtain and enjoyed the sun rays which freely played in my cubicle. In those days of celebration, even the winds promised to behave. Calculating our position every twelve minutes - instead of the usual six - was luxury to me and I entered into a new civilization of leisure.

When I jumped out of the Lancaster, at Juvincourt, close to Rheims, I don't know what stopped me from making the gesture which Pope John Paul II made so familiar: kneeling down to kiss the ground! Maybe something warned me that this would be useless. So, I just bent down and furtively caressed the soil with my fingers. I was quite surprised, as I stood up, to see that my hand was holding a pebble.

***

Then came 'Operation Dumping.' In the sheds of the airbase laid mountains of incendiary bombs which had to be disposed of. The devils were packed into our holds, and we went to ditch everything in an abyss of the North Sea. Ecologists should not pull their hair out. Our artificers had defused the bombs, and there was no risk that mud and silt would catch fire. We can trust the powers of the seabed to assimilate the most bizarre nutrients. They have no doubt long since changed our bombs into fantastic reefs where the soul of fire still sleeps. As in those underwater volcanoes which we visited - as kids - with Captain Nemo.

***

In those days I gave two talks on the BBC. 'My First Peace-Time Flight' and 'Back to Earth' but had completely forgotten about them. Back home in Mauritius, my friend Marcel Cabon insisted that I was a poet! Of course, we were all free to be poets when we were twenty, and surely there must have been something of a poet in me, but sadly I had to shoot him down to be able to grow up. I can now confess where I dropped his corpse - I mean, my manuscripts - somewhere south of the Equator, on a night bustling with wings, off an island where some venerable gentlemen had made a fortune selling bird droppings. Please don't see any naughty symbols here.

The scripts of the above talks were thus lost at sea. A good friend who had, at the time, published 'My First Peace Time Flight' in his magazine 'L'Essor,' gracefully gave me a copy. I thought that they should be included in this book although their author does not look like me anymore.

Maurice at the end of the war.

Chapter Fifteen – My First Peacetime Flight

From Little Staughton, 582 Squadron had been assigned to transport troops from Italy in a series of manoeuvres known as 'Operation Dodge'.

After a few days we headed for Bari: it was my first peacetime flight. I did not immediately realise what that meant. As the weather was awful, I shut myself in my cabin, leaned over my instruments and conscientiously calculated the effect of the wind on our course and speed. But after three hours of blind flying, having passed the bad weather belt and crossed the last cloud ridge, we suddenly emerged into clear skies, slightly south of Toulouse.

Under the aircraft, kaleidoscopic landscapes rolled on to a region where mountains, sea, and sky co-habited in radiant blueness.

I thought, to hell with navigation! The weather is too beautiful to work behind a black curtain. Moreover, what's the use of sticking to the course? Today, anti-aircraft batteries have been silenced, and all the aircraft in the vicinity are friendly ones. Let's go and wander in the light.

So, choosing the most sparkling gems in the casket of the sea, I pointed them out to our pilot. We went on a joyride from Narbonne to Marseilles, then up the Riviera at about 200 miles an hour and scrolled from the islands of Hyères to Cape Corsica. Over Sète, I leaned over to see the 'Cimetière Marin' where Valéry had just been buried. As I murmured a few of his verses to myself, Johnnie, surprised, said: *"I beg your pardon?"*

"Oh, the wind is veering, set the course to 087."

Near the island of Elba, we made a detour to see Rome and count its seven hills. For a few moments we could make out the dome of Saint Peter's Cathedral glittering like a large jewel in the morning sky.

Within two hours I had absorbed more visions and memories than I could ever have collected during a whole fortnight on the ground. I reviewed the battlefields of the Anzio[100] beaches, Monte Cassino[101], the Garigliano[102], and the Gustav Line.[103]

Between Ischia and Capri, we bore left to fly over Naples and the Vesuvius. I must admit that the bay of Naples is as beautiful as the bay of Mahebourg[104] in Mauritius!

Wishing to share those treasures with our passengers, I presented the town to a major, who had been groaning weakly for some time at every lurch of the aircraft: *"There is Naples!"* The major looked out of the porthole and saw the never-to-be-forgotten bay: He did not die but was violently sick.

We then squeezed in between two peaks of the Apennines, to come out into the plain of Foggia. Still, on a southern course, we finally saw the Adriatic Sea. For the first time after seven years, I would soon be enjoying the warmth of the sea against my limbs, smell the spray and the seaweed, and feel the salt burning my eyelids.

On the coast and warming up in the sun like a lizard, our destination, Bari gleamed ahead. Bari where I would re-discover the taste of peaches, grapes, and melons, while seven-year-old kids would try to sell us British pounds at fabulous black-market prices. Bari, where that afternoon the sun would – in a festival of light - give in to a most incredible moon while, we would listen by the pier, to the first tenor and the first mandolin.

---

[100] *Anzio is a medium-sized fishing port on the coast of Lazio, south of Rome. It was an important Roman port but is now better known as the site of an Allied landing.*
[101] *The Battle of Mont Cassino which lasted from January to May 1944, was one of the most important battles of WW2. It effectively blocked the Allies on their way to Rome but they finally won after several violent engagements.*
[102] *On 21st January 1944, the 3rd Battalion crossed the Garigliano River in Italy, to prepare for an advance northwards but enemy defences made this impossible. It held that position for fifteen days under constant shell fire, and in almost incessant rain. During this time, it regained complete control of the No-Man's Land, repelling all further counter attacks despite heavy casualties.*
[103] *The Gustav Line was a staunch defensive line built by the Germans that spanned from the Tyrrhenian Sea to the Adriatic Sea defended by fifteen German divisions. The Allies had to push through this line to open the way to Rome.*
[104] *The most spectacular bay in Mauritius at the foot of the Lion Mountain*

Tardily enough, my duties drew me back to my navigation table. I noted in my log: 14.27 Bari, and five minutes later, as the Lancaster jolted along the dusty track: 14.32 Landed in Bari. I had just completed my first peacetime flight.

Little Staughton. 22nd August 1945.

Maurice (top right) and 'Loopless' (centre left) at 582 Squadron. It is thought that the pilot (left) is Johnnie Ross-Myring.

Chapter Sixteen – Returning To Earth

Only a few shredded pieces of my BBC talk 'Returning to Earth' survive in my brain.

Remembering it all would be as vain as going back to sleep to catch a dream. I can't even find the tone which the young navigator would have used then. And so it's a 60-year old man now expressing himself, wholly unmasked.

I concede that time has made my body heavier than air, but I still feel a secret fire burning inside me which age itself cannot turn off. Elderly men often forget what happened on the previous day, but faithfully remember events more than fifty years old; days when they tasted fruits which they should not have reaped until they were mature enough. They tasted bittersweet, and today I still don't know whether I loved or hated it all.

Of course, there was that terrible anguish which clamped my whole body during certain flights over Germany. The peacetime flights, however, allowed us to see, from above, the futility of so many things for which men had been prepared to die for. Altitude sometimes gave us some very sweet breaks.

In my treasure cave, the bright snowy mornings of Manitoba - where our yellow aircraft glided on air smoother than dormant water - will shine forever. During a stormy night, there was also that opening in a chaotic sky where the sight of a tiny lantern, appearing and disappearing in the loneliness, was like a star sent by earth to give us hope.

I confess that we also stole some precious hours from the war. Sometimes, during a flight, a 'benevolent' fog or a 'friendly' thunderstorm would force our chiefs to cancel a sortie. Instead of making us play sitting ducks for seven long hours in the smelly cabin of a bomber, Luck gave us a free night off.

It was hard to stop our happiness and relief from noisily bursting out at the 'good news' Our meeting places would no longer be Essen, Cologne or Monchengladbach, but some of the nearby pubs: The Golden Lion, The Old White Swan or the Stuttering Parrot.

In our favourite pubs, a fairy had changed the volcanoes of flak into fountains of beer and wine. Again, those signs were misleading. While similar breaks would have been unimportant in peacetime, back then, they felt almost miraculous because of the perils they briefly brushed aside.

The spontaneous thrill of an aborted flight, however, seemed vain when compared to the serenity and profound joy engendered by a successful operation. After landing, I would always sip - to make the pleasure last - a burning hot rum-and-coffee. It would chase from my veins the bugs of the German night. It felt so good to be able to stretch my muscles at will, after so many hours of squatting. I would test each of my senses to see how well they had resisted the flak and the fighters; smell the fragrance which the last stars distill in the dew drops of dawn; look at the kids playing and laughing and listen to music broadcasted by 'Paris Liberé'.

The war had somehow upset my poetical values. I then found 'La Madelon'[105] prettier than 'Hérodiade' and 'La Marseillaise' more stimulating than 'La Jeune Parque!'

I could never stop gazing at the friendly faces surrounding me. Today, captured within the white edges of the runways, like framed portraits, they are very precious visions secured in the galleries of my brain.

***

After the tension of the raids, we could feel more acutely every little wave of happiness flowing over our miraculously cured planet. New units were being formed in the RAF with apparently less rigour but also less freedom. Somehow my passion for aviation dwindled in peacetime. Strangely, I felt as proud, strolling the streets of London in my brand new tweed jacket (which I still wear every time I travel to Europe), as I had had been wearing my first uniform, or even that little Navigator's wing which made me feel so lofty.

My perspectives are getting blurred, and my memory plays tricks on me. It pretends that on those days - where I was so grateful to be able to touch hard,

---

[105] *La Madelon (I'll Be True to the Whole Regiment) It speaks about soldiers flirting with a lovely young waitress in a country pub and owes its popularity to its clean lyrics at a time when army songs were generally rude. One of the most popular French songs of World War I, it remains a patriotic, well-known song in France to this day. It was revived during WW2 when Marlene Dietrich sang it in Paris on the 14th July 1939.*

solid ground with my two feet - I vaguely regretted the snares I had left lurking in the skies.

Just perfume in the breeze or a reflection on the water can suddenly allow a flow of memories to rush in. Like an ancient record which suddenly emits the most crystalline sounds, messages from the depths of my youth now have meanings I never suspected they had.

In Souillac, I often stand on the cliffs overlooking that mighty marine river which rolls its opaque currents between the Antarctic and the southern shores of Mauritius. The last rays of the sunset on the wild blue waves, glide towards me like shining pathways from a world that is no more. I then allow myself to drift, in that golden mist, towards that Other Me who travelled so far from Elsham. The other Me then says, presumably for both of us: *"Time has come to return to earth and say goodbye to everything that we once were."*

"Yes, but you know I do not need to fall asleep to see everything I viewed from the sky, and even if I don't listen, I hear, forever and ever, the rumbling noise of our four engines, taking off!"

Chapter Seventeen – Blue Grey Humour

Anyone having enough time and courage to read the vast number of books written about the Air Force at war will necessarily conclude that the life of a crew was only an uninterrupted succession of dangerous or thrilling adventures. That's inevitable, as aviators writing their memoirs will naturally highlight their most exciting or dramatic moments.

Generally, it's an illusion which has been exaggerated by the cinema. According to the numerous films that I saw about the war and which are now all mixed up in my mind, this is more or less what the average day of an airman appears to be:

7.00 to 9.00 am. After shooting down two or three Messerschmitt - before breakfast - the Hero returns, completely burnt out. He will be able to grab some sleep, at long last!

9.30 am. Alas! The Commander summons him. Faces look tense, and Churchill walks in: "Hitler has just set up a diabolical weapon. I need some volunteers for a suicide mission."

10.00 to 11.00 am. To save democracy, he cancels lunch with his fiancée. She is so upset that he won't see her brand-new low-cut dress that she decides to date an MP, well known for his punctuality.

11.00 to 12.00. After flying under bridges and zigzagging above columns of enemy tanks, the Hero succeeds in destroying the diabolical weapon. But he crashes, and his aeroplane explodes.

12.00 to 3.00 pm. He miraculously escapes and immediately takes the lead of the local 'maquis,' captures the headquarters of the Gestapo and liberates a phalanx of atomic scientists, sentenced to hard labour in Germany.

6.00 pm. Through a smart device, he manages to return to his base that very same day. Just in time!

6.05 pm. The German fighter-bombers are attacking, and all the bombers may be destroyed on the ground. With a glass of Dry Martini in one hand and an old hunting rifle in the other, he jumps across the flames and shoots the German leader down. The other raiders get scared and fly away.

7.00 pm. Full of pride, yet broken-hearted, he slowly strolls to the nearby pub to get drunk, all alone…

Things did not really happen that way. Moments of exhilaration or terror represented only a small fraction of our time – just like the tip of an iceberg. Our days were composed of many other routine tasks and distractions. Sometimes the base looked like a giant holiday camp where we leisurely strolled along the shores of Death.

In return for the comparatively few hours we spent playing heads or tails with our skins, the War Lords granted us the right to live like princes the rest of the time.

The truth might seem scandalous. As patricians, only fighting in the skies, we had a battalion of technicians to look after us, and I must unreservedly admit that we lived comfortably during the war.

Of course, there was always the cumulonimbus threatening to strangle us like boa constrictors; thick fog blurring out our landing strips; Messerschmitts or Junkers rushing at us, and flak continually devastating the sky. Above all - and this was not just a nightmare - there was the rebellious outcry of young flesh refusing to bleed to death or be charred.

The therapeutic power of time has, over the years, erased moments too painful to be stored for too long. Instead, it sheds a soothing glow on our most glorious hours, removing some of the anguish and the grief. Sometimes it feels as if life at the Squadron was full of suspense and almost thrilling due to the permanent threats which we had to resist.

As a result, when today I try to see how Adjutant Navigator Matricule 1808006 looked like, I picture myself – how ironically – more often on a bicycle than in an aircraft's cabin.

Our conservation instinct prevented us from taking the war too seriously, even when our friends were falling around us. We could not afford any spare time to mourn or bury our dead. Thus, during a raid over Germany, the escape hatch of a four-engine Lancaster suddenly opened, and an air gunner from one of the Squadron's crews was brutally ejected and crashed on the ground. As a funeral homage, his navigator composed a burlesque quatrain which became a very popular tune of Bomber Command, that season.

"We pounded old Fritz, the bounder,

With our four thousand pounder;

And when that was not enough,

Into the bargain, we threw Jimmy Duff!"

Please don't take offense and accuse him of being cynical or heartless. I knew another crew which, after a similar accident, completely broke down and had to be reformed. Jimmy Duff's crew held good: that's the whole meaning of that story.

During the war, the most decisive weapon of the RAF was neither its bombs (named after sweets or girls like 'Cookie' or 'Ten-Ton Tessie), nor those radar apparatus with bizarre appellations (I.F.F, H2S, LORAN, OBOE and not even the incredible Gee, which is probably the most fantastic toy I ever owned in my whole youth). It can now be revealed, without betraying any military secret that our mysterious weapon, that unbeatable 'trick' which allowed us to carry on, was above all the power to laugh about anything and most of all, about ourselves.

***

The personality of our Commander in Chief, Sir Arthur Harris, immensely contributed in giving us - as part of the prestigious Bomber Command - that brisk and buoyant pace with which we walked in those days.

Our Chief was one of those great leaders whose charisma attracts legends like a magnet. The media, with outdated Victorian prudence, persisted in calling him, Bomber Harris. We were not afraid to just call him, very affectionately and most respectfully, Butcher Harris!

When the venerable Admirals - gilt-edged but slightly mouldy inside - jealously tried to retain for their fleets the millions of pounds Sterling which the Butcher needed for his bombers, he publicly accused their sacrosanct battleships of being old dinosaurs. We joyously reiterated his Napoleonic apostrophe to a General, who maintained that the Infantry would always be the Queen of battles: 'Once the Air Force has destroyed its supplies and lines of communication, any army can be arrested by the Police.'

But Bomber Command would not have been Bomber Command if we had not expressed our admiration for our Boss by grossly badgering him without pity. We thus maintained that his 'Ladies and Children first' approach when bombarding towns was somehow misleading!

Although he always managed to give us the best possible food during the worse rationing periods, we would still voice our ingratitude by saying: 'Good old

Butcher, he snatches milk and oranges from babies' mouths to give them to us. He's a unique bastard!'

A wireless operator from our Squadron had composed a seditious cartoon to show how the Butcher allegedly launched the spectacular raids which he fancied so much.

In the first image, one could see the Butcher - impeccably dressed - sitting at his desk in the morning. The image of a wise and thoughtful leader, announcing to his headquarters: 'Tonight we shall send 200 bombers to Cologne.'

The second showed the Butcher finishing his lunch, with his cap slightly tilted. Looking quite pleased he announced: 'After careful consideration, let's make it 400 bombers!'

In the next image, he was spread out in an armchair near the Mess's bar. His face had turned crimson, and he had pulled off his collar and his tie. With his cap back to front and his feet skidding on a layer of empty bottles he howled: 'Damn it all! Let's make it 1,000 bombers!'

That was gross satire as directing 1000 bombers towards a single target, would have required at least three weeks of intensive work from Headquarters. We would burst out laughing and say, 'Very accurate!' But none of us would have wanted another Commander than our famous Butcher!

***

I believe that the famous thousand bomber raids[106] were probably, in fact, the most gigantic hoax of the whole war! Due to lack of appropriate equipment, most of what Bomber Command had attempted to do in 1942, proved to be a failure. Rumour had it that only about 7% of the crews engaged had actually hit their targets! That meant huge sacrifices causing only minor damage to the enemy.

For that reason, in the high spheres, it had almost been decided to abolish Bomber Command and redirect its crews to fighter squadrons, coastal defence units or transport groups. In addition to the official reasons given, the Higher Administration had possibly found a clever way of getting rid of the

---

[106] *The first of the Thousand Bomber raids in May 1942 proved excellent propaganda but required scraping together every possible aircraft from squadrons and training units alike, often with scratch crews. Within two years, however, Harris was able to launch such massive raids using all front-line aircraft and crews.*

cumbersome Butcher. That threat infuriated the Butcher even more. He had incessantly harassed the authorities and knew he was about to break through: Boffins[107] were fine-tuning radar instruments and new navigation techniques which would, at long last, allow him to manage the hitting power of Bomber Command effectively.

More importantly, despite all their mishaps, his crews still had a burning desire to fight. The spirit in Bomber Command became even more aggressive when it realised that, at that stage, no other Allied Force would have the power to carry the war into the heart of Germany.

His men (who had always been willing to fight, even for nothing, they were all volunteers) would be prepared to go to any extremes, once they saw how deeply their blows could hurt the Enemy.

In 1942, Bomber Command literally raced against time to avoid being disbanded. It is then that the Butcher organised an enormous bluff to obtain the extra time he needed to prove the value of his weapons. His plan was brilliantly simple.

One thousand is a magical figure; the year one thousand, Garibaldi and the Thousand, A Thousand and One Nights, the year two thousand etc.

Now there would be the Thousand Bomber Raid. To reach that decisive figure, old cuckoos, with damaged wings and old training aircraft, probably unable to carry a single bomb, were pulled out of their hangars just for the show. The official target was Cologne, but the Butcher's real aim was to drop on the War Ministry and the Main Head Quarters, the most prominent advertising bomb of all times.

Operation Millennium was a success. The Germans knew fear and the foe within was knocked out. Popular imagination went wild and Bomber Command, having entered the legend in just one night, could no longer be harmed by the plots hatched against it.

***

We liked Americans because they were generally nice guys who kept at least half of the German fighters busy. But they had too much money, and we could

---

[107] *Affectionate name given to scientists and engineers working on the creation of new weapons.*

not resist the pleasure of teasing those 'nouveaux-riches.' We pretended that forty American bombers attacked by German fighters, had only managed to destroy one of the enemy! As all the crews claimed to have sent the enemy fighter crashing, it was purportedly inscribed in the records of all forty crews that they had each put down a German fighter. The whole American Airforce could, therefore, boast about having destroyed forty enemy fighters in a single raid.[108]

The Fortresses, conceived for day raids, were loaded with so much defensive armament, that they could only carry two tons of bombs, while our average loads would be six tons.

To put the Americans back in their place, we invented another little riddle. We would sing the first line in a deep military baritone voice, then ululate the second line in a high-pitched soprano tone:

"We are Flying Fortresses at 40,000 Feet,

But we drop a tiny mini weeny bomb!"

We would then repeat those lines over and over again, referring to smaller and smaller "bombinettes" which were finally reduced to the size of kids' fire-crackers.

Our pilot, Johnnie, had imagined a secret trick to make our allies less boastful about the number of fighters they allegedly shot down.

He would accost an American crew and voice extraordinary admiration for the performance of their B17s. The Americans, delighted to meet a British pilot who was not out to snub them, allowed themselves to talk freely about their prowess, boasting about all their bombing feats. Johnnie, feigning total astonishment would then earnestly ask: *"Is the Fortress a bomber?"* and then smoothly throw in the supreme insult: *"I thought it was a fighter!"*

In general, our victims were fair play, and one even shouted: "Bull's eye!" But once, a pilot from Brooklyn blew up with rage and insinuated that the RAF was scared to fly to Germany in broad daylight. That was doubly unfair since our Lancasters – initially designed for night operations only - very often participated in the daylight raids, suffering heavy losses[109]. I spitefully replied that the

---

[108] *Over-claiming was indeed a problem for all sides during the war, not just the Americans.*
[109] *Lancasters were engaged in daylight operations as early as 1942, but seldom with much success. In the second half of 1944, and with the opening of the second front,*

American Air Force would order its planes to abort a mission if ever their urinals overflowed. I don't know if it was that comment, or the avenging laugh of a patriotic waitress, which set fire to the gunpowder, but there ensued a massive brawl.

Now that I have been representing law and order for so long, I should not confess that the only sport for which I was super gifted was brawling. Johnnie was a fighting animal. Despite being wrapped up in fat, Loopless Finnigan was always eager to show that, in a busy ring, his ninety-four kilos could make a difference. Our rear-gunner, Eddie was a lightweight, but his adventurous childhood in the back streets of Portsmouth had taught him how to hit below the waist. The Americans received a good beating and ran away ingloriously, while Eddie ironically invited them to a second Pearl Harbor.

On our side, there was hardly any damage. Our mechanic, Mickey Marsh, who had rushed into the fight whipping around his long thin arms - like Don Quixote tilting at the windmills - was showing an awesome black-eye. Hubert, our bomber, had a big bump on the top of his skull but Eddie maintained that this could only have resulted from hiding under a table.

For a little while, we feared the reaction of the Police, but the latter was indulgent and sent our Station Commander a toned-down report.

(For the sake of clarity, in Bomber Command a Group Captain commands a station, a Wing Commander a Squadron, and the 'Flights' are each led by a Squadron Leader. Following the same principles, we had Flying Officers who had never flown, Pilot Officers who were navigators, and Intelligence Officers who were spies!)

Our Group Captain called us, trying to look cross: *"Your behaviour is totally unacceptable between allies!"* He carefully avoided looking at me - as I should have been reprimanded - and obviously found it very hard not to burst out laughing. He added: *"OK for now but next time you go hunting Yanks, try not to make so much noise."*

As most Mauritians in the RAF, I would wear a Cross of Lorraine[110] before leaving on an operation. Occasionally, some grumpy old officers, who had no

---

daylight raids became more common, especially against the flying bomb sites, and were denoted in log books at the time in green ink.
[110] *The cross was the symbol of Joan of Arc and subsequently adopted by De Gaulle for the 'Forces Francaises Libres'*

other means of participating in the war effort, would order me to remove it since it was 'incorrect dress'.

I rebelled and haughtily replied that my family had never felt bound by what had happened in 1810, between a Corsican Usurper and an English Monarch, whose legitimacy could easily have been challenged for certifiable dementia.[111]

Often our sense of humour was not manifested through words but through deeds which were not always entirely legal.

One night, seven of us were to meet in a pub close to the airfield. Six of us, including myself just left our bicycles on the pavement, without even thinking that they might be stolen. The seventh one, Hubert, kept repeating that we were tempting the devil. He did not even trust standard padlocks and tied the front wheel of his bike to a lamppost, with a very hefty dog's chain and an extra-large padlock.

When we walked out, our six bikes stood where we had left them. The only things left from Hubert's bike were the front wheel and the chain, still solidly clinging to the lamp post! Obviously, to play a joke on Hubert, somebody had unscrewed and removed everything possible including the handlebar, the frame, rear wheel, pedals, saddle and all. Hubert never found them.

To me, the masterpiece of British humour at war was probably the Amiens affair. To divert our blows from spots which were too vulnerable, the Germans had built dummy targets. That is how far they had pushed the art of camouflage. The most striking counterfeit had been a false Berlin, complete with an artificial Spree!

The Germans had posted near Amiens, in France, a dummy squadron of Messerschmitts made of plywood. Having uncovered the ruse, the RAF was said to have sent some light bombers to attack them with wooden bombs! Although the raid was not materially productive, it was a far better boost to our morale than the destruction of several genuine military targets. Men will follow anywhere a leader capable of such superb impertinence.

That effervescence in our blood and that incredible surge of energy (after having believed for so long that our days were counted) was to culminate in the fleeting

---

[111] *This refers to the Conquest of French Mauritius by the British forces under the reigns of Napoleon I and King George III - Mad King George*

and delirious springtime of 1945. Peace exploded everywhere in an incredulous Europe.

The 'precarious hosts of the moment' that we had been - constantly treading on a thin line between life and death were suddenly discovering that we had a future. It was stretching out in front of us, and maybe some of us would die old. That thought made us high, and any stupid little joke would instantly provoke loud hilarity.

To keep us busy, HQ decided that we should take our 'Rampants' on flying tours over Germany. The RAF wanted its ground staff to see to how the equipment which they had so carefully pampered us with had been used. To let them have a good view, we would fly at low level over the devastated towns of the Ruhr.

That notorious Ruhr, where so many of us had found either glory or death. We gazed at those old volcanoes, which we had managed to kill with an even deadlier magma.

We could not talk about Death. Instead, we behaved childishly, trying to mystify our passengers with equivocal jokes. Surprisingly we were the only ones to laugh to tears, leaving them totally puzzled. I think it was impossible for them to relate to what was being shown to them or imagine what had really happened there. They could not possibly understand. Those guided visits were officially baptized 'Cook's Tours' by the RAF. To have some fun on those flights, where nothing ever happened, we had invented a new game called 'Find Hubert's Bomb.' We would pick out, far from the centre of a bombed town, an isolated crater and after several loops, we would scream: It's there! I recognise it! We would then maintain that it was our bomb aimer, Hubert, who had created that eccentric cavity with his bombs and started counting how many heads of cattle had probably perished there.

We had nicknamed Hubert 'the Cows' Attila'. Mostly for the benefit of our female tourists, Eddie would then add, in a most solemn voice: *"History will decide what role Hubert's merciless destruction of the Teutonic bovine stock played in Hitler's ultimate demise!"*

Will I soon need to pinch myself to remember that war was not just a time full of fun and laughter?

Chapter Eighteen – My Burning Home

It is impossible for me to desert Elsham. Some places take hold of your heart and never let go. From this distance, it is impossible for me to see whether any roads or rail still lead there.

When, through the deserts of the past, I return, in my mind, to the airfield, my eyes find nothing but a large empty space: like the bridge of a ship cleared for action. However, emerging from all those things that have vanished, I see faces. Faces which have stood the test of time, more durable than the asphalt of the landing strips or the corrugated iron of the barracks.

During one of my trips to England, I happened to spend a day in a village, just a few miles away from Elsham. Although I was dying to see it again, a profound instinct warned me that if I crossed the last hill hiding it from my view, a fragile charm might be broken. If ever 'my Elsham' so vividly alive to me, was brutally cut off from the roots ingrained in my memory, it might vanish like a broken dream.

After the Armistice, Elsham's airfield, which had been built for war, lost its purpose and discretely withdrew into the shadows. As if paying a ransom for its survivors, Elsham probably allowed itself to be 'bombed' by time. After 35 years, what mask is it now wearing?

I guess our barracks have been demolished long ago and the control tower dismantled too. What about the Club where the members of the Zoo used to meet to discuss their wildest dreams? Does its shadow still survive?

All this does not matter anyway. Elsham was much more than just a few acres of land crisscrossed by three runways; it was the home of a special team, brought together for a joint mission. It might not have survived the day on which its occupants had to pack their bags.

I do not think that any tourist will ever find 'our' Elsham behind that hill. I will not walk there as I do not want to run the risk finding a field of cabbages or beets where Runway Number 1 once used to be. I am sure, however, that the airfield still finds proper shelter in the minds of those who once had the right to use the land as they pleased.

For a long time, I believed that whenever any members of the Squadron would meet again, wherever that might be, Elsham would be revived. I did not know then, that we would need a password.

A Ghanaian navigator[112] I knew in Elsham, once came to Mauritius and asked to see me. He was an incredibly charming man who had been, for some time, his country's Ambassador to Moscow. He was a born storyteller, and his talent gave Soviet bureaucracy an almost ridiculous, yet amusing dimension.

But when we parted, I bit my tongue just in time not to say: *"So happy to have met you!"* A voice inside me incessantly asked: 'Why does he pretend to be Kodjoe and act as if I was Maurice?'

There was an unbridgeable abyss between those two young lions who had sharpened their claws on Germany's back, and what we had become. Sharing common memories felt more like discussing a film we had seen, rather than an adventure we had shared.

The imposter was finally unmasked when I took him to Gris-Gris, in Souillac. I wanted to show him that amazing beach amidst the cliffs, where nature has surpassed the most beautiful creations of landscapers.

On our way back, he climbed the stairs, one by one. He did not bounce from one step to another. Undoubtedly, he could not be Kodjoe! But I was climbing slowly too, so it could not be me either!

***

A few weeks later, a young lady called me and said: 'You don't know me as I wasn't born at the time. I am the daughter of your good friend M...' When I saw her, I thought to myself: 'Old pal, how come you have such a beautiful daughter?'

But this time the passwords matched, and the transmutation worked. M's daughter had the same smile, accent, and gestures of her father. I was instantly transported to Elsham and time no longer mattered to me.

I then understood that there was no point in looking for runways from which I had flown or in flying the latitudes, longitudes, and altitudes which I had noted in my logbook. Unattainable by helicopter or submarine, Elsham had become an island which could only be reached through a time machine.

***

---

[112] *Kodjoe was one of only a handful of Africans to serve in the RAF outside of the South African Air Force (SAAF) in the Second World War.*

Some adventures follow me by day and haunt me by night. The images that fill up my dreams do not dissipate when I wake up. Like the wavelets of the incoming tide, they keep flooding my soul with memories. I cannot count how many of my nights were only memories from Elsham! They are always there, claiming their fair share of me.

Often, when I'm still half awake, I receive a call. A voice I once knew whispers: 'Jump out of your bed now and go running under the stars, on roads freed from the bustle of the day. Out there, where memories go hand-in-hand with portends, you'll find the strength to spread your wings and fly again. Or, was it only the aeroplane's engines that allowed you to soar? Maybe you'll finally be able to understand the significance of those missions which could not be divulged because they were unfinished.'

These calls only last a few of those microseconds which I used to measure with my radar instruments. I have never been quick enough to slide into the gaps which they open in the citadels of my nights. I keep on training. I like to think that I am getting better and maybe, one day, I'll dive in.

***

On those nights, reminiscence always takes me back to Elsham, through tiny alleys, only known to my team and me. The place has aged but not changed. My bicycle still leans against the wall of the station, but I no longer need to ride it.

I gently surrender to the soft breeze and allow myself to glide in low pass around the perimeter. Very soon, other shadows will join me in the luminous zone where I am evolving.

Names and faces lost to the fever of those days, but resting in my heart, under impalpable broken columns, suddenly come to life again. I find it quite natural to see Gilbert walking by my side. Sometimes it is Smithie and sometimes both of them. Except for the fact that they will be forever young, nothing allows me to distinguish between those who were lost and those who survived.

Whenever we meet, it is those young heroes - who preceded us into places where the living cannot enter – who, strengthened by experiences they cannot yet share, gently keep watch over us as big brothers would.

Tacitly, we have agreed to always meet in the open as what we fought for was freedom. If someone inadvertently decided to close a door, the frail structure in which we still survive might crumble like dust.

The light which bathes the landscape looks likes daylight, but we would be disappointed if the stars were absent from the sky. No need to look up to know they are where they ought to be, twinkling discretely.

From the horizon, gliding towards us are the beautifully fresh and blushing faces of the girls we once knew. I can see better from farther away; it must be distance and time, added to the alchemy of my dreams, which have in my heart, immortalised Elsham.

The Force which pulls me there has another purpose than just allowing me to revive my adolescence. I am yearning to finish, together with my friends, a mission for which we were united, but unfortunately failed to complete. My interminable training and too many sleepless nights only allowed me to catch the war by the tail. I could not do much but am still convinced that those long insomnias have probably helped me to navigate through the pitfalls of what is now called 'Peace.'

Some of my decisions find their significance and their source in things which moved me then. In those days, every spare minute granted to me held the promise of a future I furiously desired even though there was no guarantee that it would be given to me.

Endorsing risk has taken me through perilous pathways where my life was sometimes threatened[113], but I always felt guided by the soldier I once was. In order not to betray him, I have tried to be entirely faithful to the principles which allowed me, during that terrible war, to cross the fire.

***

On the day I said goodbye to my friends from the Zoo, there was a heavy silence. We were all waiting for words which never came. We had been raised to a privileged position - allowing us to become visionaries. As we parted, there was suddenly an impalpable feeling that our eyes might be too weak to keep gazing at the sun.

We had been warned: no one acting selfishly would ever grab the evanescent truths lurking in the skies. At any time, everything could be lost if some reckless guy tried to highjack, for himself, the blessings destined to the Squadron.

We knew that the secret code, which we had started to decipher at the Zoo, would only be revealed if we remained bound by ties stronger than Death.

---

[113] *In his later career, Maurice received no fewer than 300 death threats.*

***

Unfortunately, we could not stop our Order of Chivalry from being dismantled. By failing to promise that we would never disappoint those who trusted us, the valiant bunch of brothers we had become, allowed our secrets to disintegrate. If only we had all agreed to meet in twenty years. Mature, but enthusiastic still, we could have rekindled, in one another, the flames of the past.

In this world, where transcendence is quietly being assassinated, we could have built incredible power plants to rejuvenate in our souls the virtues of altitude and azure. In the four corners of our planet, we would have created magic places where our souls might have found peace.

***

I cannot imagine that my friends do not feel the same scorching desire to return, with eyes wide open, to that place where so many lives were lost at dawn. I was blessed to find my way home and will forever be grateful to those who allowed me to survive and gave me the chance to discover how blue the sky can be beyond the clouds.

Epilogue

With the conclusion of hostilities, Maurice stayed in the UK to read Law, finishing second overall in the Commonwealth final bar exams. On returning to Mauritius he became a district magistrate and subsequently held the posts of Master and Registrar of the Supreme Court of Mauritius. He was Director of Public Prosecutions during the race riots that preceded independence in 1968 and later Chief Justice of Mauritius, often acting as the island's Governor General. He was knighted by Queen Elizabeth II in 1978. After his retirement, he succeeded Princess Alexandra as the first Mauritian Chancellor of the University of Mauritius.

Among his many achievements, Sir Maurice presided over the first Commission of Enquiry on Drug Trafficking which helped to dismantle – albeit temporarily – the most important drug cartels in Mauritius but led to a series of threats on his life. He was then asked by the Government of Mauritius to become its non-elected Attorney General/Minister of Justice. In that role he enabled two important laws to be passed: one restoring the right for Mauritians to hold multiple nationalities and the other abolishing the death penalty (with the exception of those found guilty of large-scale drug trafficking).

Although passionate about Classical and Contemporary Literature, he was also a keen fan of Harry Potter, and wrote four books of his own. He was a founder member and President of Racing Club of Mauritius and President of the Mauritius Sports Association. He died in 2004, on the 9 November – the anniversary of De Gaulle's death - surrounded by all his family. The traditional homage delivered by the Supreme Court after the death of a judge was the first to be delivered in French since the English captured Mauritius in 1810.

Maurice and his wife outside Buckingham Palace to receive his knighthood.

(L) Maurice with the Prime Minister Sir Seewoosagur Ramgoolam after he was appointed Ag. Governor General. (R) As Chief Judge of Mauritius.

Maurice's final resting place.

Addenda

Maurice Rault – Operational Record

Crew

Pilot Officer 'Johnnie' F Ross-Myring

Sergeant F C 'Mickey' Marsh

Sergeant H 'Hubert' R Bretherwick

Sergeant L J M Rault

Sergeant G 'Loopless' Finnegan

Flight Sergeant G J 'Neville' Nevill

Sergeant M E 'Eddie' A'Court

OPERATIONS (officially recorded)[114]

March 7/8   Dassau – Johnnie flew as a 'second dickey' with Flight Lieutenant C H Short RCAF.

March 18/19   Hanau

An operation of seven hours and ten minutes. Attack involved 277 Lancaster and eight Mosquitoes from 1 and 8 Groups and was highly accurate. Most of the towns historic buildings were hit and more than 2,000 people perished. Light heavy flak was encountered although no searchlights. Fighters were active over the target. Only one Lancaster was lost, a 103 Squadron Lancaster of Flying Officer Essex.

---

[114] *There is a suggestion that Maurice flew several other trips as a spare bod that were not recorded.*

March 21   Bremen (daylight)

An operation of four hours and forty minutes. This was a comparatively small raid comprising just 139 aircraft to attack the Deutsche Vacuum oil refinery. Conditions over the target were almost perfect and all of the crews were able to bomb visually. No aircraft were lost though this was fortunate, for six Squadron aircraft were hit by a barrage of heavy, concentrated flak. One of the pilots, Flight Lieutenant Wilson, was wounded in the head and landed at Kirmington.

March 22   Hildesheim (daylight)

An operation of five hours and fifteen minutes involving 238 aircraft. The target was the railway yards although the attack morphed into what became something of an area attack. Great swathes of the town were destroyed in what was the only attack of the war on Hildesheim. Its great cathedral was burned to the ground and more than 1,500 killed. Crews reported that the bombing was concentrated and there was little or no flak. Four Lancasters were lost.

March 24   Harpenerweg (daylight)

Another daylight operation of five and a half hours duration. The target was the Benzol plant near Dortmund involving 185 Lancasters and Mosquitoes divided between Harpenerweg and the Matthias Stinnes plant at Bottrop. The main danger came from predicted flak which damaged a number of Squadron aircraft. Three Lancasters were lost though all of the 103 Squadron crews returned without any casualties.

Losses recorded by 103 Squadron in March 1945

1/2nd March 1945

F/O Alexander Thomson RAFVR – KIA

F/O Frederick Brickman RAFVR - KIA

Sgt R C Pain – POW

P/O John Peace RAFVR- KIA

F/S William Tromp RAFVR - KIA

F/S Alan Crampin RAFVR - KIA

F/S John Rochester RCAF - KIA

F/S John Grice RAAF - KIA

5/6th March 1945 - Chemnitz

F/O Gordon Exel RCAF - KIA

Sgt G H Wilson RAFVR - PoW

F/O Michael Griffin RCAF- KIA

F/O J H McKenna RCAF - PoW

F/S F P Monaghan RAFVR - PoW

F/S J L Cooke RCAF - PoW

W/O D King RAFVR - PoW

F/L Max Norem RAFVR - KIA
F/O Keith Jackson RNZAF - KIA
F/O George Taylor RAFVR - KIA
F/S Jack Wright RAFVR - KIA
F/S John Green RAFVR - KIA
F/O Frank Elliott DFM RAFVR - KIA
Sgt Robert Brown RAFVR - KIA
Sgt Walter Seeckts RAFVR - KIA

7/8th March 1945

F/O Samuel Saxe RCAF - KIA
Sgt J J Bent - PoW
F/S Robert Leavers - KIA
F/O Michael Shatzky RCAF - KIA
F/S Keith McGinn RAAF - KIA
W/O A L Cruickshank RCAF - PoW
F/S Reginald Snell RCAF - PoW

F/O William Havell RAFVR - KIA
Sgt James Roy RAFVR - KIA
Sgt Joseph Smith - KIA
F/S Norman Mayo RAFVR - KIA
Sgt Geoffrey Burch RAFVR - KIA
Sgt Arthur Whyte - KIA
Sgt Arthur Fry RAFVR – PoW. Murdered in Captivity.

F/O William Nightingale RCAF

Sgt H S Simpson RAFVR - Safe

F/S R A Almas RCAF - Safe

F/S R Magahay RCAF - Injured. Safe

Sgt D Strickland RAFVR - Safe

F/S J A Goldie RCAF – Safe

F/S J A Hawreliak RCAF – Injured. Safe.

12th March 1945 - Dortmund

P/O B F Wright RCAF

F/S G R Tracy RCAF

W/O J Coulson RAFVR

Sgt B Heath RAFVR

F/S K Coleman RAFVR

F/S A J Bocinfuso RCAF

Aircraft was hit by a 250lb bomb which embedded in the wing. Crew all bailed out safely with the exception of Sgt Francis Carter the Flight Engineer who pulled his rip cord too quickly and the parachute failed to deploy.

12/13th March 1945 - Op Minelaying Kullen Sound.

S/L Stan Slater DSO DFC RAFVR - Evaded

Sgt K Foster - Evaded

P/O M H Bertie RAAF - Evaded

F/O H A S Mitchell RAAF - Evaded

W/O T Fairclough RAFVR - Evaded

F/S Harvey Porter RAAF - KIA

Sgt Donald Morris RAFVR - KIA

16/17th March 1945 - Nuremberg

F/O E W Armour RCAF – PoW
F/S E Young RAFVR – PoW
F/O A R McKenzie RCAF – PoW
F/S J H McRoberts RCAF – PoW
Sgt William Fox RAFVR – KIA
F/S J B McCormick RCAF – PoW
F/S J D Smith RCAF – PoW

F/L Arthur Stepharnoff RCAF - KIA
Sgt John Grant RAFVR - KIA
W/O Rowland Parks RCAF - KIA
P/O Harry Stott RAFVR - KIA
F/S Alan Davies RAFVR - KIA
F/S Wilfred Whitehead RAFVR - KIA
F/S Robert Wilkinson RAFVR - KIA

F/L Alastair Watt RCAF - KIA
Sgt Jim Jackson - KIA
F/Sgt Bill Fetherston - KIA
F/Sgt George Blackshaw - KIA
F/Sgt Stan Hickey - KIA
F/Sgt Al Bellisle RCAF - PoW
F/Sgt Al Wotherspoon RCAF - KIA

18/19th March 1945 – Hanau

F/O Adrian Essex - KIA

Sgt Charles Gregory - KIA

Sgt Walter Jewiss – KIA

F/S Albert Whiteing – KIA

Sgt Stanley Armitage – KIA

Sgt James Aldridge – KIA

Sgt Leonard Pendleton - KIA

Sources:

Bomber Command Losses – Volume 6 – 1945 – W R Chorley

AIR27/817 ORB 103 Squadron March 1945

David Fell of the 103 Squadron Association

https://www.northlincsweb.net/103Sqn/html/103_sqn_losses_index_1944_to_1945.html

Acknowledgements

The cover of the original, French language, edition of this book, published in July 1985 by Best Graphics Ltd., Port Louis, Ille Maurice.

I wish to express my gratitude to Caroline Anne Rault, Dagmar and Celeste Lamaletie, Marie Josee and Mike Craig, Alain Bancilhon, Monica Maurel (my English teacher) and Dr. Serge Maurice for their precious advice, comments and encouragement.

Special thanks to Bob Whymark and David Fell for sharing their knowledge, info and appreciation and to Sean Feast without whose help those memories might have perished in a Cloud somewhere.

In addition, the authors would like to thank Tracey Turner of the Manitoba Historical Society for putting us in touch with Bill Hillman and Greg Gigurdson of the Commonwealth Air Training Plan Museum (www.airmuseum.ca) who were most helpful in finding photographs to illustrate Maurice's time at 7AOS. They collectively do a fantastic job in keeping the memory of Portage La Prairie and Canada's contribution to the air war alive.

Danielle Lagesse.

Danielle and some of her team.

Printed in Poland
by Amazon Fulfillment
Poland Sp. z o.o., Wrocław